EVERYTHING TO LOSE

NEIL BAKEWELL
EVERYTHING TO LOSE

metro

Published by Metro Publishing
an imprint of John Blake Publishing Ltd
3 Bramber Court, 2 Bramber Road,
London W14 9PB, England

www.johnblakepublishing.co.uk

First published in paperback in 2010

ISBN: 978 1 84454 977 1

British Library Cataloguing-in-Publication Data:

A catalogue record for this book is available from the British Library.

Design by www.envydesign.co.uk

Printed in Great Britain by CPI Bookmarque, Croydon, CR0 4TD

1 3 5 7 9 10 8 6 4 2

Papers used by John Blake Publishing are natural, recyclable products
made from wood grown in sustainable forests. The manufacturing
processes conform to the environmental regulations of the
country of origin.

Every attempt has been made to contact the relevant copyright-holders,
but some were unobtainable. We would be grateful if the appropriate
people could contact us.

To my wife, Jennie, for all her love and support, even when I didn't deserve it. You can cancel the JCB now!

CONTENTS

1

THE HORRIFYING REALISATION

'If we do nothing, you'll be dead in less than five years.'

The words from the doctor hit me like a thunderbolt between the eyes. Five years? When you're only 32 years old, being dead within five years isn't really an appealing prospect. I was in this position because over the last 20 years I had fought, but lost, a battle with a terrible addiction to food.

Knowing you are fat is one of life's less pleasant feelings. Being classed as obese takes that feeling a step further: you start to feel dirty. Let's face it, there is no dirtier word in the English language at present than obesity. And being morbidly obese is another stage further down the line. Falling into the morbidly obese category is really degrading and, in addition to near-constant breathlessness, pain in the knees and back, increased sweating and skin conditions such as boils, you also worry about becoming another *Daily Mail* story about people who have had to get the fire brigade out to rescue them from off the toilet. However, as bad as these conditions are, they are nothing compared to the feeling of being told that I was super morbidly obese. Until I was told this piece of information, I didn't know such a state existed. Unfortunately it does, and I sit unequivocally in that classification. Quite frankly, it's both humiliating and frightening.

I was at St Richard's Hospital in Chichester for an appointment with Mr Shaw Somers, probably the leading obesity surgeon in the country. I was hoping to find out whether I would be eligible to undergo obesity surgery in order to help me lose weight. I had always had a weight problem to one degree or another, but, over the last couple of years, frankly, the situation had become stupid. I didn't know how much I actually weighed, having long ago outgrown a set of bathroom scales. Being 6ft 5in, I knew it was going to be a big number, but I was appalled when I was told that my weight was a staggering 43 stone.

The solution to my problem and the horrifying prognosis on my life expectancy was a gastric bypass, a major operation that, because of my weight, could kill me.

I had become used to feelings of depression over the years. As I rose from being obese, to morbidly obese to super morbidly obese, these feelings only got worse. It's hard to explain how someone in my situation really feels. Unfortunately, in the world we live in today, people are very quick to judge. The obese are quickly becoming some of the most hated members of society. Fat people are commonly considered to be greedy, lazy and stupid, and many people think that we are deaf. But trust me, my hearing is sound and I can hear every comment and insult that is spoken about me in hushed voices. Insults and stares have become a way of life. Step by step, I have found myself retreating further and further away from mainstream society as I hide away from view. Of course, this simply compounds the problem further.

I am angry at everyone: my wife, my family – but principally myself. I'm an intelligent man, I have a degree in Aeronautical Engineering. I have burning ambition – I really want to make a success of myself. I have desire, passion and a hardworking nature. But here I am, 32 years old, 43 stone and eating myself to an early grave – a very early grave – without fulfilling my hopes and dreams. Why can't I control myself? I know that takeaways, crisps and chocolate are killing me, but still I stuff them in. Why?

If I knew the answer to that question, then I guess I wouldn't be in this appalling situation. My other overriding emotion is that of humiliation. I am a failure. Any success or happiness I may have enjoyed is overshadowed by my condition. It's not easy to put into words how it feels to have your whole life controlled by your size. Going out is a problem – the cinema, the theatre, even restaurants – because the seats simply aren't big enough to accommodate me. I have to drive the biggest car available on the market. I have to look for parking spaces right next to the place I am going to because I'm simply unable to walk very far.

I don't look for sympathy, just understanding. People in all walks of life experience problems of one kind or another. People become drug addicts, alcoholics, smokers, gamblers or shopaholics. My own problem and addiction is with food. I have lived with this problem all my life, but the time came for me to battle back and try to defeat the demons that consumed me.

Saturday, 24 August 2008 – Consultation Day

We arrived at St Richard's the customary two hours early. Guess it was a sign of my nerves that I didn't want to be late.

To sum up the whole day's experience in one word – SHOCK!

I don't think the seriousness of my situation hit me before today. Now, however, it's hit me squarely between the eyes.

My weight is an astounding 43 stone – how the hell can it be that much? That's the weight of people on telly. People who have been bed-bound for the last six years and get pizza posted to them through the letter box by the delivery boy. How could I have let myself get in this f***ing condition?

St Richard's has its own special bariatric department that specifically treats obesity and its related issues. In the reception area, they have special bariatric chairs designed for the larger person. A family of three sat in the chair next to me – I comfortably filled mine.

Next shock: Shaw Somers tells me I have just five years to live. That just hit me like nothing before. My wife, Jennie, of course, is in tears. I was simply numb.

The gastric bypass operation is what I was dreading but, if I'm honest, it was what I was expecting. It means cutting my lower intestine and sewing it further up on the stomach. The stomach is then stapled in order to create a small stomach pouch which will be about the size of an egg. This is classed as major surgery. Of course, I came wanting just a gastric band, not a major refit of my internal organs. But Shaw tells me that the danger is not in what he does to me while I'm under general anaesthetic – but putting me to sleep in the first place.

This, of course, is because I weigh so much. I am at the high-risk end of the scale of dying either during the operation or just afterwards. The official rates are one in a hundred but with me being a higher weight my chances have to be less than that. However, everyone tells me that I am young, have a normal blood pressure, no diabetes and a good heart (hopefully), so this all has to be in my favour. I am a worrier – that's my major problem, it will play on my mind now for weeks.

I accept that there is no real alternative to this operation, although half my mind still tells me that I can lose this weight on my own. However, the evidence of the last 15 years is against me. Even if I lost a few stone, there is no way I can shift over 20 stone on my own.

So – five days in hospital, the risk of a heart attack and death but the benefit of losing around two stone a month. It's a difficult balancing act.

Immediately I realise that the less I weigh on the operating table the greater my chances. So I've got to try to lose as much as possible before the operation.

Shaw seems pretty keen for me to have the surgery and I get the impression that if he could he'd be wheeling me down to the theatre this afternoon.

However, there is a slight problem. For a while now I have suspected that I have suffered from sleep apnoea (a sleeping disorder characterised by pauses in breathing during sleep). After explaining my symptoms to Shaw, he seems to agree that I am suffering. This is a problem that needs sorting out before he can risk an operation – sleep apnoea weakens the heart and increases the chances of complications.

So the timescale is this – about a month to get the sleep apnoea condition assessed, and then, if I do have it, around two or three months of treatment and then the operation. So this means I have around three months to try to get some weight off me. Surely I can get four or five stone off me by then.

They also want to film me for a documentary series called Fat Doctor *to go out on TV. This means exposing my life to the general public – it's difficult to decide what to do. I guess that, in the end, we will end up agreeing to do this.*

Jennie, who must have been feeling just as bad as me after the appointment, is completely and utterly great. She is feeling extremely positive and thinks that this is really the way forward for long-term success for me. She tells me how our lives will change completely and she's right. At the moment our lives are pretty dire – I need to do this as much for her as for me.

Jennie rings the family to explain what is happening. I am a little bit teary-eyed and can't face doing it myself. I do speak to them all later on when I regain a bit of my composure and they all tell me that I have no choice but to have the operation.

They are right.

I just hope it's the right choice.

2
CHILDHOOD

I was born Neil Edward Bakewell, at a few minutes after 6pm on 7 June 1976 at Burton District Hospital. England were batting in the Test Match and my father had to be called away because of the birth, much, I'm sure, to his disgruntlement. My mother, Carol, was a secretary and my father, John, was a personnel manager at one of the leading breweries that was based in the beer Mecca that was Burton-on-Trent. When I was born, the midwife told my mother that I had hands like a boxer and feet like a policeman. An early indication, perhaps, that I was going to become a big bloke.

We lived in a relatively modern semi-detached house in a nice area of Burton. However, I have no memories of living there because when I was two my parents divorced.

So I lived my childhood with my mother. I understand

that we spent a while living with my mother's mother, my gran, in Carlton Street, a typical road in Burton-on-Trent filled with Victorian terraced housing. I have few memories of this period, other than sleeping in my bedroom. The bed was an old single wooden thing, big, sturdy and sustainable on which my gran seemed to have placed about three different mattresses, making it the tallest bed in the world. I virtually had to climb up it at night. The room also had some kind of strange ventilation system built into the brickwork, and at some stage during the previous hundred years someone had stuck an old sack into it to stop the draughts getting in but on a windy night the sack would flap about, causing me nightmares. The other thing I remember about that house was the floor in the living room. It was completely uneven. I have no idea what it was made of but it was amazing playing with toy cars on that floor, pushing them up and down. How my gran never tripped over and killed herself I'll never know.

Then me and my mother moved to a similar property in nearby Calais Road. The first day at the house I managed to fall down the concrete steps in the garden. I completely messed up both my knees and elbows and I got a piece of grit stuck in my hand. My mother battled for over an hour with a sharp needle with me screaming to get that piece of grit out. She never managed it and today I can still see it, a small black dot, in the base of my right hand. I remember my mother and her friends redecorating my bedroom, hanging great wallpaper with aeroplanes on it. This, coupled with a duvet with the cockpit of a Spitfire on it, meant I dreamed of being a pilot when I grew up.

When I was five, I started to go to school at Horninglow Infants, an old school about a mile's walk from our house. Mum and I walked every day – very healthy, but also because we didn't own a car. The building dated from 1876 and still had the old boys and girls entrances with the names carved into the stone above each door. My mother and my grandfather had both attended the school, and little had changed since their schooldays: high-tech it was not. It was very large, very formal and very Victorian. In fact, it could have featured in a Dickens novel. It did have one fabulous feature though, in addition to two large playgrounds and a smaller undercover play area – it had a secret garden. In an age where playing fields and playgrounds were fast disappearing, this was amazing for a youngster. It was a complete garden, accessed through a large red wooden door with a big round metal handle, and had a massive lawn surrounded by a tall stone wall. It was complete with a climbing frame and other play equipment. On hot summer days, we would be allowed to spend our lunchtime and break times in it. Bliss!

My mother has a picture of me as one of the three

kings in the school nativity play. Looking at the picture today, my little chubby cheeks stand out a mile. I wouldn't say that I was fat, although maybe the signs of my forthcoming problems were evident. I have to say at this point that my mother always fed me healthy, wholesome home-cooked food. There was no junk food, no takeaways and far from a constant supply of sweets or chocolate – for me, these would come later.

The school had its fair share of quite rough kids and, like many children, I went through a period of being bullied. A couple of kids would pin me against the wall while others took turns to kick my shins. I don't know why I was the one who was singled out for this sort of treatment. I used to go home with bruises all over my legs. Despite my mother asking what was going on, I never told her. I can't remember how or why it stopped. Maybe when I moved on and left to go to junior school.

I saw my father on Saturdays. He would pick me up in the morning and, together with my new stepmother, Helen, we would go to my nan and granddad's house. My father was very into cricket, playing for local teams all his life. We used to play for hours in the back yard, using the old well-worn bat that Nan kept in her shed and an old bucket for stumps. As the yard was brick, if you pitched the ball just right on one of the uneven cracks you could get it to turn a mile. On Saturdays at Nan's the biscuit tin was always open and I would quite freely help myself. This was the first time I remember having open access to food, and it was a feeling I liked. Nan and Granddad would always send me home with a little bag of two or three chocolate bars which I would eat after school during the week as a treat.

My grandfather wasn't a well man. He had been a caretaker at the school over the road from where they lived now and then worked at one of the bottling factories in the town. He had suffered from gout and as a result at some stage had been forced to have some of his toes amputated. He was a quiet man and a little gruff in nature at times, but he was always kind to me. I got a shock one day when I came home from school, my mother sat me on the sofa and told me that Dad had been on the phone and that unfortunately Granddad had died. I had a very odd reaction. I paused for a few seconds, and then asked my mother what was for tea – I didn't shed a tear. This wasn't because I wasn't upset, it was just my way of dealing with the news. Apparently, Granddad had been sitting in his chair by the table and simply had a massive heart attack, no pain – the best possible way. I didn't go to the funeral, I didn't want to. Again, this was my way of dealing with things, trying to disconnect myself from the problem.

I was seven years old and the time had come for me to start junior school. Unfortunately, I immediately came down with chicken pox, which meant that I was unable to start at the new school at the same time as my new classmates. My first day was three days later than everyone else. I had to stand up in front of the class and say who I was and why I'd been off. I didn't like everyone looking at me. My school was William Hutson Junior School and it was a far more pleasant building than the Victorian infant school. It had big wide corridors, classrooms with large windows, playing fields and it even had an upstairs. I had lots of friends and I used to enjoy going to school. Without brothers or sisters of my own, it was great for meeting children of my own age.

Then we started having PE lessons with Mr Bold. Mr Bold was quite an elderly teacher who taught one of the third-year classes. Mr Bold specifically took us for gym lessons. Now, gym lessons never have at any stage in my life been my forte. Mr Bold was a very strict, uncompromising sort of guy. I used to dread those gym lessons, simply because I couldn't do anything. Handstands, cartwheels, forward rolls and backward rolls, each was as badly executed as the last. I'd keep on moving to the back of the line in order to avoid my turn. Then one lesson I was spotted, singled out and made to do a forward roll in front of the group. I couldn't do it and for my trouble I was called 'a big fat baby' by our wonderful teacher, right in front of the class. This is the first time I can recall ever being called fat. I'd never really considered my appearance before, but, yes, I guess if I look at photographs of the time you could see that I was a little overweight. Nothing staggering, but I was certainly fatter than the other kids, but I was also taller than the majority of them as well.

I don't really know why I was fatter than my classmates; certainly my diet at home was nothing less than healthy. I didn't eat a lot of vegetables at that age but then not many kids did, and I loved fruit. There was zero junk food in my diet. I'd never even heard of burgers, pizza or Indian food at this stage in my life. The only factor that I can think of is exercise. Maybe I didn't get a lot of exercise at that early age. I got a lift to and from school from a friend of Mum so I never got the benefit of walking to school. Also, with no siblings I didn't play outside as much as I could. We lived on a main road which prevented any playing of football or stuff in the street with other kids. But on the other hand I had a bike which I rode round and round our block all the time. I'm sure genetics also played a part. My father was very stocky, while my mum was always on one diet or another. It may just be that I have one of those bodies that likes to hold on to its fat reserves.

The PE incident really put me off school for a while. I tried every trick in the book to get out of school on PE days. It never worked; my mother was not one for her son to miss school. Her favourite line, which I still quote back to her today, was 'You'll feel all right once you get with your friends.' I also produced a classic incident in the school Christmas play, a performance of the show *Trig Trog*. Somehow the nativity was sandwiched into this story and I had landed the role of Joseph. At the end of the play, Mary, who was sitting on a stool, was meant to stand up, I was to pick up the stool and we were both to walk off the stage. Of course, at the end of the play, Mary went to stand up, I pulled away the stool and for some inexplicable reason she sat back down. The stool wasn't there and she landed hard on the stage, to the great amusement of the audience. Anyway, the girl in question didn't hold it against me and she was to become one of my best friends in my teenage years.

Sunday, 25 August 2008

Didn't sleep at all well last night, everything was racing through my head. Mind you, I never do sleep well these days. It will be interesting to see if I do have sleep apnoea, it would explain a lot about why I'm so bloody tired all the time. And it would shut Jennie up a bit if I have a real medical condition.

My feelings of fear haven't disappeared at all overnight. Just think, in less than three months I could be lying on an operating table. Worse still, the operation could be over and I could be lying on a mortuary slab. I must make every effort to lose weight. I've got to stick at it. It's only going to be for a few months. If I can shed a few stone prior to the operation, it can only help my chances of survival.

I get the Alpen out for breakfast. I actually quite like it so it isn't really a hardship. I just have to watch my portion sizes, that's all.

I'm a little bit confused by all the literature I've been given, everything seems to be contradicting itself. I'm pretty certain that Mr Somers said that there was a 1 in 20 chance of dying, but according to the paperwork it's only 1 in 100. I guess my chances are worse because I'm heavier. It's got to take more to knock me out than it would do an average-sized person and the more anaesthetic you have the harder the burden on the heart.

I doze on the sofa, as per most of my weekends... and my evenings....and time at work if I think hard enough about it without falling off again. I must have sleep apnoea. I snore like a trooper and at times wake up gasping for breath, so I think it's pretty much a given. This is good because it means the operation will be delayed and there will be an opportunity to lose more weight beforehand.

Sundays are so boring these days because I'm so incapable of doing any walking. Me, Jennie and her daughter Jodie can't go anywhere or do anything. It would be fantastic to be able to just go out for a decent walk and blow out a few cobwebs but it's impossible when the best I can do is walk about 40 yards. Jennie is very frustrated by it all as well, she is so moody on Sundays. I guess it's because she's already had a Saturday lying in front of the box and another day of it isn't very appealing – especially when she has to do all the washing as well. It takes her so long because my clothes are all so big. At least once I've had the op and lost a load of weight Oxfam will be pleased, they can have my T-shirts to use as emergency tents for disaster zones.

Cheese salad for lunch. Again, I like salad. So why don't I eat more of the stuff? It took me about eight minutes to put that together. When I ring up the kebab shop it takes longer than that to explain what I want because the bloke's English is so abysmal. Maybe if I stick really hard to healthy eating and eat smaller portions then I could lose the weight by myself – I'm sure other people have done it, so why not me? That's got to be the best option. I really can't see me coming through this operation. Surely I can do this myself.

When I raise this with Jennie, she tells me I'm an idiot or words to such effect. I haven't managed to lose weight before so I'm hardly going to start now, am I? She does say that she will help me lose weight for the operation – but I've got to have the operation done. Not just for me but for her and Jodie as well.

I know she is right. But I hate that feeling of failure and lack of self-control. It makes me feel useless.

3

STUTTERING SOLUTION

Many people hate the dentists but not me because I spent so long in there as a kid. This is not because I didn't brush my teeth and they were full of holes – no, I'm quite proud of the fact that even today I don't have a single filling. I needed a number of braces to straighten my teeth, nothing major, just quite a lot of little things. The big problem was that one of my front teeth wasn't coming through after the milk tooth had fallen out. After a year of being called 'toothy', I was sent for x-rays and it was found that I had an extra 'floating' tooth in the gum stopping the front tooth coming down. This meant an overnight stay in hospital and an operation to have it removed. It was simple enough and I still have the offending tooth in a little jar somewhere. Fortunately, this solved the problem and the new tooth duly appeared, so I was able to smile in school photographs again.

One thing that still strikes me about my early childhood is Christmas. My mother may not have had a lot of spare money but I certainly didn't go short at Christmas time. Gran would stay the night on Christmas Eve and we would lay out a sherry and mince pie for Santa before going to bed. I was never one of those kids who was up at five o'clock ripping open presents; in fact, often Mum would have to wake me up on Christmas morning. Then she would go downstairs first and sneak open the door at the bottom that concealed the staircase and express gasps of astonishment at the fact that Father Christmas had visited and left us all presents. The living-room floor would be filled with parcels and packets of different sizes and shapes. I always got one major present and then lots of little ones and I got lots of gifts from my mother's friends. Dad always bought me a nice big sack of goodies too. Christmas dinner was always turkey with all the trimmings. At an early age I was never that keen on the dinner itself. I liked the Christmas pudding, though, and all the chocolate figures on the tree, which was an artificial one that came out year after year, with the same decorations. Then in the evening it was turkey sandwiches in front of the telly. There was nothing like Christmas.

When I was nine, something happened that probably shaped the rest of my life. Overnight, as if by a curse of witchcraft, I developed a stutter. This stutter was so bad that I couldn't even string a sentence together. It was very similar to that of Gareth Gates when he was competing in *Pop Idol*. The impact that living with a stutter had on my life was mind blowing. Children can be cruel and I can assure you that in my case they most certainly were. I was mocked and laughed at every time I opened my mouth. So I did the obvious thing, I hid away and stopped talking. I stopped participating in lessons at school and I avoided talking in the playground.

The worst experience was when I was asked by my teacher to nip down the corridor to the next class and borrow a pair of scissors. I sometimes question my teacher's motive for sending me to do this task, but I think what she was trying to do was to get me speaking again. I walked down the corridor like a condemned man going to the gallows. I kept repeating out loud the sentence that I wanted to say. 'Can Mrs Ife borrow a pair of scissors please, can Mrs Ife borrow a pair of scissors please.' I wanted to ensure that I got it right first time and without any stuttering. Of course, when I got to the classroom, the inevitable happened. I just couldn't get the words out, I stuttered and spluttered as my face twisted and contorted and got redder and redder as I tried to force the words out. Thirty nine-year-old children burst into rapturous laughter. Unfortunately, the teacher concerned was pretty appalling at controlling a class and the kids continued to laugh and hoot at me. One boy was even standing on a table doing an impression of my humiliation. I kept on smiling and laughing, just treating it all like it was a big joke, but inside I was broken.

My mother soon stepped in and we began going to weekly speech-therapy sessions. Slowly, week by week, they managed to get things sorted out and my stutter began to get better. One of the tasks I had to do was say a simple sentence like 'The cat sat on the mat' very slowly, over a 20-second period, slurring one word into the next. Try it, it's so hard and you feel like a bit of an idiot. It took a relativity short period of around eight months to get me speaking near to normal again. The stutter wasn't gone completely, but at least I could now speak normally the majority of the time, just getting stuck on occasional words, much like Arkwright on *Open All Hours*.

But this period of my life had a real and profound effect on me. My confidence and outgoing personality had been shattered and it would take a long time before these were restored. I could now speak reasonably normally, but in high-stress situations, like talking in front of a group, the stutter was profoundly more prominent. This caused me to go to extreme lengths to avoid doing things. For example, one morning we had a class assembly during which I had a short passage to read out. The passage was handwritten and every time we practised I messed it up on purpose, pretending I couldn't read the writing. Eventually the teacher got fed up and I joined the backstage crew.

My mum was very pleased that my rehabilitation had come on so much that I was now speaking in an assembly, so I lied to her and made out that I was still doing it. One of my mother's friends went to the performance and word got back to Mum – she hit the roof and she didn't speak to me for about three days. I think after this incident the teachers decided not to push me into speaking in public. Therefore, I was given the role of chief tree in the end-of-term production. It wasn't a complicated role, to be fair – my face was sticking out of a cardboard cut-out of a tree and I had to wave my arms a couple of times during the play. As 'chief' tree, I also had to lead the dance that the trees had to perform. Strangely, my Oscar nomination never came.

I had been a member of the beaver scouts since I was six years old and at this time the beavers' football team was going great guns. The previous year, we had been hammered in every game 9–1 and the like. However, this year, it was our turn to give out the hammerings. We won the league and cup without a single game lost. Of course, the pictures showed that my top looked a lot tighter than anyone else's. It was great being part of a team, especially as we were winning things. I lived for the matches at the weekends.

Mum had started working again and had a job as an assistant in the pathology lab at the hospital. This meant that I let myself in when I got home from school, about half an hour before she got home. As a result, I was alone with food at my disposal and I was at a very low ebb because of my stutter. I remember breaking down one night in my mother's arms and telling her how useless I was at everything. The first thing I turned to when feeling down was the biscuit tin. I realised that a Club biscuit and a couple of custard creams each day after school weren't missed. I liked the thought of doing something that no one else knew I was doing, so, every day, I would come home from school and raid the biscuit tin. This started off a lifelong habit of secret eating.

I had a bit of a shock one day when I came home from school. I was all excited about being placed in the top set for everything in my forthcoming term at my new secondary school. My mother was at home talking to a strange woman. I was immediately dispatched upstairs out of earshot. It turned out that she was a social worker who was calling about Gran whose health had been failing over the last few years. She had suffered from diabetes ever since my grandfather died, when my mum was only 19 years old. Gran had always managed the condition well, but became a little forgetful and started forgetting to take her pills. Unfortunately, this forgetfulness was the sign of something more sinister. The word was never mentioned back then, I was merely told that 'Gran was going a bit funny'. The medical fact was she was suffering from dementia. As Mum now worked, I used to go round to Gran's during the holidays. If I'm honest, it was very boring, as I had none of my stuff there so the holidays were a nightmare for me. I was often glad to be back at school so that I had something meaningful to do. Finally, one holiday, I managed to persuade Mum that I would only go round to Gran's for my lunch. Sadly, Gran's condition was getting worse and Mum strongly suspected that she forgot to eat, which of course was bad for her diabetes. One day I went round and she didn't have any proper food in the fridge. For lunch she decided we would share a pork chop and a packet of crisps. This was not normal and was a result of her dementia. I could tell something wasn't quite right, as she was acting kind of odd. Suddenly she just collapsed. I managed to catch her and it was a good job I did because the floor was tiled and she could have had a nasty fall. I sat her on the kitchen step and rushed round for one of the neighbours – known to me as Auntie Joyce. She charged round and went straight for the sugar pot and gave Gran a great big spoonful. Gran had suffered from a diabetic hypo, an episode of low blood sugar which has caused her to temporarily lose consciousness. It was clear that she could no longer look after herself so the social worker was paying a visit to my mum to discuss the options for Gran's long-term care. I remember Gran having to spend a short period in hospital, probably after another hypo, and then afterwards she never went back home but went into a nursing home instead.

When it was time for me to start secondary school, my stutter was fortunately much improved. It really only came out in high-pressure, high-stress situations, so I learned to avoid these as much as I could, or else do my best to prepare for them. The school was right next to the junior school and I continued to catch the same lift in the morning. My mother was very keen on me having the complete correct uniform and wouldn't listen to my appeals that a blazer wasn't required. Therefore, I turned up on the first day as one of about six kids in the entire school dressed in a blazer. Starting a new school as 'blazer boy' wasn't overly conducive to confidence-building and the thing lasted about three days until it got stuffed in my bag outside the front door and put on again when I came home.

Another change was about to happen in my life – my mum was about to meet Pete.

Sunday, 25 August 2008

I've been sticking to this diet religiously, it's like praying to the altar of fruit and vegetables. Assuming I've got sleep apnoea, which I must have, then I'll have three to four months to lose weight. If I can shift eight stone in that time, which would only be two stone a month, then they might say that I don't need to have the operation – and if I do I'm sure to stand a better chance of survival.

I've even declined a takeaway! We came home tonight and I really couldn't be bothered cooking so Jennie and Jo had an Indian. I simply had a tuna salad and bloody nice it was too. Or at least that is what I told myself as the chicken tikka masala was shovelled on to a heavenly bed of rice right in front of me. To be honest, they did say that having a takeaway wasn't fair, but we only had enough salad left for one and I really wasn't cooking.

When I diet, my thoughts are solely about food, normally strange fantasies about cooked breakfasts. I do love a good cooked breakfast – bacon, sausage, fried egg, beans, mushrooms, hash browns and loads of lovely toast, it makes my mouth water just to think about it! Buffet breakfasts at hotels are the best, you can go up as often as you like. If I have the operation, I'll never be able to have one again. If I control what I eat and lose weight without the operation, then occasionally, just occasionally, I'll be able to partake.

Everywhere I go I see food. I get out of the car at work and the smell from the sandwich van tempts me to transgress. When I get inside, someone is eating a yogurt, and then a client wants a nutrition course. The TV seems to be showing nothing but Marks and Spencer delights! I was never a pudding man but a glance at their chocolate sponge dessert makes me salivate. Then the next thing I see is Gordon Ramsay showing us all how to cook. Everywhere I turn, food is flung in my face. Or maybe that's just my perception.

If I have to have the operation, then all of this will be gone. What will I replace it with? I don't know whether I will be able to cope. After all, food has been my friend and my support for years, it will feel like a divorce. I'm not sure if this is what worries me the most – maybe it's not really the fear of dying. After all if I do die I wouldn't feel anything, would I? Maybe this enforced removal is what my big concern is – not having the freedom, or simply the ability, to go and eat what the hell I want.

But if I can lose enough weight, then 'bang', the need for the operation and fear of any kind will be gone.

4

TEENAGE YEARS

I was 12 years old when my mum met Pete. She'd been on her own for ten years and she started going out to singles nights with her friend from over the road, who was a widower. I had no problem with this at all. I really wanted Mum to find someone. I didn't want her to be alone when I was eventually old enough to leave home. When they went out, I would go across the road to stay with my mum's friend's children, who were slightly older than me. It was always good to spend time with people of a similar age, especially for the legs of darts in the front room and the overs of cricket in the yard.

It was at one of these nights out that Pete appeared on the scene. Suddenly, flowers started arriving at the door and I knew that something was happening. He was witty and fun to be around. It was fair to say that I took to Pete straight away. However, I must admit I was a little shocked when two months later my mother told me she was getting married. In fact, it was a little more than shock – I burst into tears.

They didn't hang around on the wedding arrangements, clearly neither of them believed in long engagements. Some four months later I was leading my mother up the aisle. When she asked me to give her away, I burst into tears again. It seemed to be the season for it. At 12 years old, you do feel a bit of an idiot dressed in a lounge suit leading your mother out of the house in a bridal outfit.

We moved into Pete's house in Barton-under-Needwood, a village about five miles outside of Burton. This presented a problem with schooling and was my only concern about the situation. Barton had its own popular school just up the road, but I wanted to continue attending my old school with my friends. Staying at my old school was something I did dig my heels in about, as there was no way I wanted to start again somewhere new. Mum had recently swapped jobs at the laboratory and was now secretary to the pathologist so her job was still in Burton, which meant this didn't prove to be too much of a problem as she would be going in to Burton anyway. After the schooling issue was sorted out, I was quite happy, especially after I managed to negotiate getting a hi-fi stacking system for my new bedroom.

Pete lived with his father, an 80-year-old former Co-op manager called Roland who, after a short while, I called Granddad. On one of the first occasions we had a dinner there, sometime before the wedding, I was astounded at how many potatoes Pete and Granddad managed to put away in one sitting, I swear I had never seen so many in one bowl. This is where I developed my taste for two pounds of spuds with every meal. However, despite my amazement at the carbohydrate consumption, I was even more astounded when I was given a small amount of wine with my dinner! I literally fell off my chair when Granddad kept on topping up my glass when Mum and Pete were in the kitchen.

Pete was very into crown green bowls and played in the first team for the village club. Consequently, I started playing as well. Crown green bowls doesn't exactly sound like a riotous sport and doesn't quite have the glamour of Formula 1, but it was surprising how many young people actually played the sport in those days. The Burton area has masses of players and there are bowls greens popping up in the most unlikely of places. Crown green bowls isn't the game you see played by formal ladies and gentlemen in white trousers on the telly – that's flat green. In crown green bowls anything goes: there's shouting and chanting from around the side of the green, people run up and down the green chasing their bowls as they make their way towards the jack. I've seen many an argument that I thought was going to end up in fisticuffs. Of course I didn't start out in the first team; I played my first season in the Wednesday-night midweek league mainly playing against fellow beginners. The following season the club started a C team for the main Saturday-afternoon league and I was selected for that. Bowls would become a fixture in my teenage years and I would play as often as I got the opportunity.

While bowls was amazingly good exercise, it did introduce a problem that wasn't going to help my weight at all. I was starting to develop a love of fizzy drinks. At home, Mum would regulate this by buying only one bottle of pop per week. It was cheap supermarket-brand cola which was never allowed to go in the fridge and wasn't nearly as appetising as 'the real thing', the black nectar Coca-Cola served ice cold at the club. That was divine. All my life I've been a naturally hot person; while other people are feeling cold and wearing a nice thick jumper, I'd be in a T-shirt, opening the window to get a bit of air in. I'd get into Pete's car and the back window would start to steam up straight away – he called me 'Hot Neck'. Because of this, I was always thirsty and could drink enough fluid to sink the *Titanic*. So at bowls matches, a bit of exercise (and it's surprising how much exercise you do get at a bowls match) coupled with the hot sun and I'd be sweating for England. Consequently, I craved a long, cool, swing of Coke. I drank it by the pint and didn't stop at just one or two. By the end of a Saturday bowls match, I'd probably consumed five or six. It was where most of my pocket money went. The amount of sugar and caffeine that was going into my body was terrible, I'm surprised I wasn't bouncing off the walls on a Saturday night.

School was progressing well. I was in the top set for every subject and was getting good marks. My blazer-boy image hadn't stuck and I had developed a wide network of friends. I decided to stop taking sandwiches in for lunch and have school dinners instead, as all my friends were having this so it seemed to be the logical thing to do. But in truth this was a fateful step. Armed with my £1 coin, I could purchase such delights as sausage and chips or burgers, things that were never served at home. I would try not to eat chips every day, because, let's face it, I knew they weren't healthy. Some kids would eat them day-in day-out and they would be as thin as rakes. I bet they are still as thin as rakes today. At that age, I didn't like any food that was sloppy or anything that had even a vaguely foreign-sounding name, so this didn't help my range of options. In reality, it was either something with chips or a roast meat with roast potatoes.

We'd always play football at break times, although

bizarrely balls were banned in the playground and so we would play with a crunched-up drinks can. These caused numerous holes in my shoes and the soles regularly came off, leading to rudimentary repair jobs with superglue and lectures from Mum. I did quite enjoy sports but PE lessons were a little bit harrowing. My school was a large one and there were about 300 kids in each year. The year group was split into two, each half doing PE on different days, which meant having to change and then shower afterwards in front of around 80 other boys. By this stage it was pretty obvious that I was fatter than most of the other kids, not to extreme levels but I was clearly carrying a stone or so extra. After our first ever PE lesson, we all paraded through the shower and one genius in all his naked glory managed to slip and fall over on the wet tiles in front of everyone, to great hoots of laughter – that genius was, of course, me. In a group of 80 boys, puberty hits at different times. While I wouldn't say that I was really a late developer, I most certainly wasn't one of the first either. This made getting changed for PE very disconcerting, my fat little undeveloped body getting changed next to some hairy brute of a kid who spoke in a deeper voice than Brian Blessed.

A highly embarrassing incident happened at Christmas at the end of that first year. The deputy head, Mrs King, came round to each class to wish everyone a happy Christmas, quite a nice touch – apart from the throwaway line 'Mind what you eat, we don't want a load of fat people here next year.'

Everyone in the class turned round and looked at me and laughed. I went bright red.

Mrs King realised her mistake and attempted to correct it with the words 'Oh, you're Father Christmas size, that's all right.'

Of course it wasn't all right – that clumsy extra line just made the situation worse.

The family came back from a few days in Yarmouth one school holiday to some bad news. We had only been home an hour or so when the phone rang. Gran had had a heart attack in the nursing home and it was looking pretty bad. We rushed down to the nursing home where I decided to wait in the car, as I didn't want to be around in case the worst happened, and with lots of medical staff around I would only be in the way. A nurse came out to the car with a glass of squash for me, and told me that Gran was very ill – I had a little cry to myself alone in the backseat. After an hour or so, an ambulance arrived to take Gran to hospital. It seemed that the doctor who was called after the heart attack expected Gran to die pretty quickly, but after she showed signs of improvement took the decision to move her to hospital to give her the best possible chance. She managed to fight for a few days but eventually she didn't have the strength any more and just faded away.

I didn't go the funeral. I had a scout camp on the Isle of Wight and Mum didn't want me to miss that. She said that Gran would have wanted me to go and enjoy myself. Scouts was something that really helped build my confidence over the years. I had been in the scout movement since the age of six, being the first ever beaver scout in the Burton area, and I moved up from beavers into cubs. The scout movement is often criticised today and numbers are falling fast, but I never found it anything less than brilliant. Camping offered a chance for outdoor adventure – there was no better feeling than sleeping under canvas. I've lost count of the number of nights I spent camping when I was I teenager, but it must have been hundreds.

When I started camping, it was the days of patrol tents, great big green things that would take about four hours to put up and would comfortably sleep six. Each morning, we would have to rig the sides of the tent in order to let in air and stop the thing going mouldy. Those were also the days of proper groundsheets; you had to ensure that the 'sod cloth' (which we all found amusingly named) went underneath your groundsheet, otherwise when it rained you and your sleeping bag were going to get very wet indeed.

I was always a fussy eater as a kid. I never ate gravy, for

example, and as a result I hated anything that I would describe as wet. This proved difficult when camping because the staple foods were things like stew – slap everything in a big pot and off you go. Other kids lapped up baked beans so this was another camp staple, but I was repulsed by them and simply passed. I may have been hungry but this lack of consumption did mean one good thing: I didn't have to pay a visit to the chemical toilet during the week-long stay. Camp toilets were not the most pleasant of things, especially when the weather was hot. I avoided them like the plague. When I got home from camp, the first thing I would always do was run to the loo.

Scouts is character building and it gives you a certain amount of leadership experience and responsibility. I was quickly made an assistant patrol leader, before moving up to patrol leader of the newly formed Otter patrol. I always made sure that my patrol was the best turned out and smartest on inspections. I always found the inspections in cubs very funny – three things were checked: if you had your name in your cap; if you had clean hands; and if you had a handkerchief with you. But in scouts the focus of inspection was more on appearance, just like the army. Learning to put a beret on for the first time was entertaining and many a scout looked like Benny Hill for the first few weeks. Berets were always very effective weapons, as they would be used as a whip, striking your opponent with the metal badge that stuck out of them.

As I got older, getting a uniform to fit me became increasingly difficult. In the cubs, as I approached the leaving age for scouts, I was described as the biggest cub scout in the world. Towards the end of my scouting career, I had to shoehorn myself into my scout trousers. Tight trousers were a fact of life for me. I always had to get trousers a waist size bigger in order to fit my thighs into them. I'd like to say it was my fine set of quads that were the problem but I guess it wasn't.

Looking back, the only thing that I can really put my weight down to was lack of exercise. I had a lift to and from school, which was sensible as I was attending a school ten miles from home. And with no friends in the village I wasn't going out playing football or other sports in the evenings. I did go to scouts on a Tuesday night but, other than a few energy-release games at the start, it was hardly an extensive workout. Games of football in the yard at school were relatively short and, again, not a great deal of energy was expended. In the winter months when I wasn't playing bowls, my exercise regime was very limited indeed.

I decided to try to do something about my weight and it was because of this that I started to go weight training. Me and my friend Matthew joined the local council-run leisure centre and we would work out every Saturday morning. The gym wasn't like modern facilities – for one thing there was no treadmill and only one stationary bike. But cardio activity wasn't the principal reason for attending. The idea was to get bodies similar to Arnold Schwarzenegger's – of course, it really didn't work out that way at all. It did give me the grounding for a solid body, which stood me in good stead when playing American football in later years, but in no way did it change my waist size or my amount of fat.

I also started playing squash. I was introduced to the game by my dad and we would play on the Saturdays that he saw me. By this time, Dad had moved down to Essex as Helen's work had taken them down there. He had got a job in London and commuted in every day. Because of the distance, I obviously couldn't see him every week. But when I did get to visit, we would go and play squash. At first I could barely get near the ball but began to get better and began to give Dad a really good game. I wanted to play more often so I also began to play with Matt on some Sunday afternoons. It was a great game which I loved and later on played it in the sixth form at school. With my previous experience of the sport and the power I had built up from weight training, no one could touch me on the court. I'd never really excelled at sport but being the one firmly in charge on the squash court made me feel good and certainly increased my confidence.

I tried my best to moderate my eating, especially when

in public, so I stopped having school dinners, and I normally just took a packet of crisps, an apple and drink to school for lunch. Crisps were not the healthiest choice but there wasn't a kid at school who didn't eat a packet of crisps with their packed lunch. With these measures, the sport and a bit of a growth spurt that took my height to 6ft 5in, I managed to tighten my belt by a few notches.

Now, I confess that there was an ulterior motive in trying to get my weight in check. A young lady had attracted my eye. It was in our special Friday-morning sessions that me and this girl were thrust together. I forget the actual title of these sessions, no doubt some crazy acronym that no one ever understood. The idea was that you did six weeks on one project then rotated round to mix with other groups of students to do something else. This particular session involved us producing a school newspaper. Me and the girl in question, Lucy, were sent over to our lower school to write a story. We got on extremely well and she managed to make the effort to laugh at all my appalling jokes which I took to be a very good sign. Now, a 15-year-old boy who has never had a relationship with a girl before doesn't have the confidence to leap straight into things, so I decided to take the slow route to wooing her. My plan was simple and subtle, well, not quite so subtle on reflection. Every Friday morning we'd sit down to write our masterpiece of creative journalism, or rather she would and I would spend the morning rubbing my leg up and down hers. Any fool would have realised that, as there was no objection to this approach and much staring into my eyes, the girl might be interested; however, it still took me eight weeks to finally ask her out. This, of course, was a watershed moment and like most teenage relationships was negotiated via a string of different friends before the final monumental nervous asking of the question. At 15, you don't take a girl out for a meal so we went for a walk round the washlands, the riverside meadows that served as the romantic backdrop to many Burton teenagers' first liaisons. After three hours, it was safe to say that my snogging technique had come on in leaps and bounds.

Mum was now working slightly later hours and so Pete always brought me home from school before going out again half an hour later to fetch her from work. One day we walked through the door and had a horrifying discovery – Granddad was dead on the sofa. This was a terrible shock, especially for Pete who had only just left him 20 minutes beforehand.

This meant I was left in the house completely on my own after school while Pete went to pick up Mum from the hospital. This was bad. During my time alone, I started eating cheese sandwiches and loads of digestive biscuits with butter and cheese. Why I started this I don't know, maybe I was bored. Or maybe I felt uncomfortable in the house on my own, which was definitely the case a few months after Granddad's death when we were burgled while away on holiday. Maybe it was that I felt comforted by the food, it's hard to tell. One thing is for sure, once I started this practice I didn't stop – it had become a habit. Every time Mum and Pete went out, I was downstairs going through the fridge, raiding the biscuit tin or opening bags of crisps – anything I could get my hands on. So this meant that in fact I was having two evening meals because we would sit down to dinner about an hour after my mum got home.

This particular increase in eating didn't have much of an effect on my weight, as it was summer and the bowls season. I'd now managed to get myself promoted to the second team and was knocking on the door of first-team selection. I also played in our Derby league side that played about twice a week, as well as the parks team that played on a Wednesday. I had also been selected to play for Derbyshire juniors and the East Midlands junior team which played about once a month. All this meant that I was playing bowls practically seven days a week. This certainly constituted a lot of exercise. There were a lot of younger players in our team, and we would run bowls in and stomp and shout. It wasn't what you might call a leisurely game for old men.

It was at this time that I noticed that quite a few girls seemed to have taken an interest in me. I was still seeing Lucy at the time and therefore declined a number of advances, including an interesting encounter in the school dark room with a girl. However, it came to my attention that Eleanor had developed a little crush on me. Eleanor had knocked me back before I started seeing Lucy and I have to confess I still held a flame for her. So quite clumsily and without a great deal of tact, I parted ways with Lucy and started to see Eleanor.

To put it simply, I was besotted with Eleanor. She had a strange, quirky personality that I found infectious. I was a little bit like a rabbit trapped in headlights. This however wasn't good, as my GCSE exams were coming up and coming up fast. My mum certainly felt that I might become distracted. I was an intelligent young man and there was no doubt I would be returning to school to do A-levels. We left school for study leave; however, this caused another problem – I was at home, doing no exercise during the day, just bowling in the evenings. Doing revision is not what you might describe as an exciting activity in a teenager's life, so what did I do whenever boredom struck? I went downstairs and fixed myself something to eat. Moreover, it was a stressful time. Teenagers were under a lot of pressure to do well even back then, and I found food a comfort. When I was eating, I was happy, relaxed and felt like I could cope with anything. It was my answer to both boredom and stress.

After the GCSE exams came and went, I had a great summer hanging out with Eleanor, playing squash and going weight training with Matthew. A group of us also had a brilliant few days away staying in a youth hostel at Boggle Hole, on the Yorkshire coast. As youth hostels didn't offer the most salubrious accommodation in those days, me and Matthew shared a bunk bed – it was here that we honed a well-worked Fletcher and Godber from *Porridge* routine.

As summer drew to a close I went down to stay with Dad and Helen in Billericay. I'd done this for a number of years. Dad would take a week off work and we would do loads of different things, such as tennis, golf, tourist stuff in London and of course the Test Match. Every year we would go to the Friday Oval Test Match. I remember the very first year we went, Dad didn't want to be late and I think we arrived at the ground at the same time as the stewards – it was a long old day. I loved every minute of it, especially as we were fortunate that there was never a day's rain during the entire tournament. It was something we did every year, up till last year when it was simply too much for me to get there or fit in the seats.

There was no danger of not getting enough exercise when at Dad's; the station was a good mile walk up a very steep hill and the park for tennis and golf was even further. Then in the evening I'd take Oscar, their boxer dog, out for a walk. Sometimes we would spend a week on holiday as well, such as to Arcachon on the Atlantic coast in France. Here a restaurant owner seemed to think that we were German and insisted on greeting us with 'Guten tag!' when we arrived, even though the rest of the conversations were held in English. Maybe my father just looked German.

This year was slightly different as I was expecting my GCSE results and was somewhat tense. The results were posted home, and fortunately I had passed the lot, not in an overly spectacular fashion: one A, four Bs and five Cs – but at least I had passed every exam I'd sat.

So this meant I returned to sixth form at school. I had chosen to do maths, physics and geography at A-level, and then everyone also had to do general studies. The leap from GCSE to A-level was very hard, especially in physics, and I found it very tough going. The overeating had begun to take its toll and my waist had increased over the summer, so aged 16 for the first time I had to get 40-inch-waist trousers. But I was so tall and well built that I carried it well.

At this stage in my life, I thought I might like to join the RAF, not as a pilot but as a fighter controller. Fighter controllers guide aircraft on their respective missions. Think of the big map with checkers being pushed about by ladies with long sticks in old black-and-white movies and the guy in charge above them with a range of telephones at his disposal to shout 'Scramble!' at some squadron, and you aren't a million miles away. However, there was the problem of passing a fitness programme and getting my weight check before I could make the move in to training.

My secret eating continued relentlessly. When Mum and Pete were out, while eating I would ring Eleanor. She was very worried about what I was consuming and told me that I was going to eat myself into the grave. I just laughed it off and told her she was being silly. If she couldn't get through to me, then no one was going to. So, when Mum and Pete sat me down one evening to express their concern at my ballooning weight, they weren't going to have a lot of success. My mum was very upset and just didn't know why I was continually piling on the pounds. Unfortunately, at that age, anything your parents say goes in one ear and out the other and you think that they don't have a clue anyway. My mother's concern didn't do anything to halt my problems – if anything, my natural reaction was typical rebellious teenager: I ate more just to spite them.

It was at this point in my life that Dad and Helen received some pretty devastating news. Helen was diagnosed with breast cancer and so started to undergo treatment. I had no experience of this terrible disease and when I heard the word cancer my first instinct was to fear the worst. Helen went through a period of chemotherapy and lost her hair but after a few months the signs were that the disease was being beaten.

However, I was soon to be knocked off my stride again. Eleanor decided that the time was right to bring our relationship to a close. I of course disagreed. To say this had a major effect on me is a complete understatement. I was completely and utterly besotted with her, but there was nothing I could do to make her change her mind. So, like any sensible 17-year-old, I did the obvious thing and completely ignored her, which created all sorts of tensions within our group of friends. Another girl showed a pretty keen interest in me – the same girl that I pulled the stool away from when she was Mary and I was Joseph – but there was no way I was interested in another relationship at that stage. I fell into a prolonged low mood and ate myself stupid. During school holidays, I would take a stroll up to the village 'to get some air' when what I was actually doing was buying large slabs of dairy milk chocolate and then eating them in an one afternoon. I'd then stuff myself silly all over again when Pete went out to pick up Mum. I was standing on the precipice, peering over the edge. I was always careful, though; I never took so much in one go that it would be noticeable. If I made a sandwich, I would always carefully wipe down the sides, ensuring that no crumbs were left. A secret eater soon learns how to cover their tracks.

Things didn't help when I passed my driving test and got my own car. For an early 18th-birthday present, Mum and Pete and Dad and Helen clubbed together and bought me a car. A first car is an amazing thing for any young man to possess and I was no different. It was a Mini Metro, quite funny under the circumstances. I would drop off Mum in the morning and go to school, then drive back home in the evening. Now I was upwardly mobile, the world was my oyster. Unfortunately, the major benefit I found for the car was not to improve my social diary but to feed my demons. With a car, a whole new world of food-related opportunities presented themselves. Drive-through McDonald's were accessible – I'd only ever eaten a couple of McDonald's meals in the past, but now I could enjoy their delightful range of products at my leisure. Fish and chip shops were also widely accessible, especially after venture scouts on a Tuesday night. Then of course there were service stations. Cars had to be filled up with petrol, after all, and, when you went inside to pay, a whole selection of tasty goodies presented themselves: pork pies, sausage rolls, crisps and chocolate bars were all consumed with the same gusto.

Monday, 1 September 2008

Jennie's birthday. I feel really bad because we can't do anything. A normal couple would be off down the local restaurant for a nice romantic meal. But the chairs are completely unsuitable, they look as if they will fall over if I even breathe in their general direction, let alone sit in them. We used to go to the theatre or the pictures a lot, now both of those are out of the question as well.

She puts on a brave face, but I know she would much rather be dressing up to go out than sat at home with a Chinese watching reruns of One Foot in the Grave. *It goes through my mind, and not for the first time, what would happen if she left me? She only has one life and she is currently wasting it on me. I wouldn't blame her if she did go – it's no life living with me. Poor Jodie must be as ashamed as hell when I drop her at school, a massive great big fat man sat in the car in front of all her friends – poor kid.*

Unfortunately, the diet has gone for a burton. I did my normal trick, I was excellent for a week or so and then bit by bit the normal ways seem to be creeping back in, so it's a Chinese tonight. As it's a special occasion I go the whole hog: chilli chicken wings, spare ribs, sweet and sour chicken, fried rice and the big bag of prawn crackers. It was great waiting for it to arrive, anticipating the smells and the flavours. It was even better while I was eating it, as it was my first Chinese for a long time and I was savouring it and making sure that none went to waste. Then afterwards I felt like shit. I was a complete and utter tosser! What was I doing? How many calories were in that meal? God knows! Don't I realise that every time I eat crap like this I'm hammering another nail in the coffin. The answer, of course, is yes, I do know that, but the desire to eat, to indulge and to gorge wins hands down each and every time.

It not the first time I have transgressed. I just can't get food out of my mind, it's only so long that I can mentally hold out. I've sent the boys at work out to the bacon-sandwich van a few times, I'm not happy with a normal bacon sarnie, though, am I? I have to get a double! Why? A throwback to 'Big Neil' at Uni I guess, always being pushed into having the biggest portion available. That's the other thing, I can't even get my own crap to eat, I have to send one of the staff because I can't walk over there!

I just wish there was a place I could go, an island or something, where all temptation was physically removed from harm's way. I suppose somewhere like a rehabilitation centre, where they sort out addictions, but, as I unfortunately don't have the income of a rock star, that is out of the question. It does make you think though: the NHS spends a fortune on obesity-related illnesses but seems to excel at coming up with stupid ideas to help you lose weight. Eat a bit less and exercise a bit more – very helpful thanks! Why not create a place for people like me to go for six months to really get to grips with my problem. In six months, with physiological counselling, fitness coaches and various treatments I bet I would lose 12 stone and break my bond with food. Of course this is all fantasy, nothing like this exists nor is it likely to. After all, fat people are a blight on society – why not let them rot in their own foulness?

I shouldn't rant, but it does upset me. At least I do have the operation – as little as I am looking forward to it. If it doesn't kill me, it will cure me.

We went straight to sleep again tonight. No prospect of getting up to the normal activities of young married people on their birthdays. I have no sexual appetite whatsoever, even if it were physically possible. Another reason why my marriage might break down. If she does walk out, where would that leave me? On the scrap heap I guess, although to be fair I feel as if I'm already there!

5

MY FRIEND FOOD

At times, my size proved useful. I remember an incident where a girl in our sixth form had collapsed in an epileptic fit on one of the building's two flights of stairs. Cue a sense of impending doom as the bell was about to ring and signal 600 stampeding teenagers about to make their way up the stairs where the young girl lay. I was grabbed from the common room to stand and control the 'traffic' – a fact my best man later related at my wedding, saying how 'I straddled the double doors like the Colossus of Rhodes while demanding of the horde of marauding teenagers in front of me, "What part of no do you not understand?"'

My stature lead me to a variety of roles in sixth-form drama productions. Appearing as a beefy lumberjack in our version of the classic Monty Python sketch was a standard role for me, maybe less obvious was as a ballerina in the pantomime we performed to the younger pupils – although the latter may well have got more laughs. The following year, I appeared as myself, Neil 'The Dump Truck' Bakewell, the legendary undefeated Sumo wrestling champion. This was not the only incident in my life that would involve Sumo wrestlers – but more of that later.

When I left school for study leave to prepare for A-level exams, I experienced the same issues as during the run-up to my GCSEs. As soon as boredom hit, I'd be off downstairs finding something to feed my face with or I'd nip out to buy more chocolate delights. Of course, I'd always be careful to hide this food in my jacket or trouser pockets before smuggling it in and squirreling it away upstairs.

The question I asked myself at the time, and have asked thousands of times since, was why am I doing this to myself. I have no real answers. There are three things that I identified as possibly being at the route of the problem. Firstly, loneliness: so often in my childhood and teenage years I felt isolated and alone. I had no brothers or sisters, which I always regretted, as living with someone else of a similar age would have been a much more sociable experience. Also, living in a completely different area from my school friends was very difficult, especially in school holidays. Secondly, boredom: I find it very hard to concentrate on one thing for very long as my mind always flicks about from one thing to another. Couple this with the feelings of isolation, and boredom strikes quickly. Finally, I was miserable: dumped by my girlfriend and under severe stress with A-level exams coming up fast and university places at stake. Food was my friend, my soulmate and my counsellor. When I was eating I wasn't alone. It filled my time so I wasn't bored and, most importantly, when I was eating I was happy. Happiness is something that everyone craves, especially angst-filled teenagers. Sadly, the happiness was only short-lived, because when I stopped eating the misery, pain and hurt crept back in.

My destructive lifestyle rapidly affected my waistline. My weight gain was so rapid I got terrible bright-red stretch marks across my whole stomach, bum and inner arms. The stretch marks on my stomach were so bad that it looked like a cat had repeatedly clawed away at my flesh, leaving deep bloody scratches. You would have thought that this obvious problem would have been the wake-up call that I needed. But unfortunately that wasn't to be.

I managed to scrape through my A-levels. I didn't get the grades I needed for my university place but fortunately they accepted me anyway. So in a few months I was going to be leaving home to go to Loughborough University to study Aeronautical Engineering. This did excite me, the prospect of living away from home with all the freedom and opportunity that that brings.

The school had arranged a leaving ball, with smart dress a must. By this time my weight had increased so much that I could no longer go out and buy clothes from a 'normal' store. I had to go and pay a visit to a shop called Mr Big in Derby in order to get my 44-inch waist trousers and outsized jacket. It was great to have clothing that actually fitted me for a change but not so thrilling to have to walk through the middle of Derby city centre with the words 'Mr Big' emblazoned on my carrier bags.

During the summer, I got a job working in a beer-packaging factory. It was tough physical work and should have done wonders for my figure. It would have done if the cafe outside the factory gates didn't sell hot sausage rolls. It was shift work which was especially tough going. I didn't mind the morning shift, 6am to 2pm, which was pretty good because it meant that you had the whole of the afternoon and evening off. But I found the 2pm to 10pm shift a nightmare. It seemed to stretch forever. It wasn't what I would describe as the most rewarding job in the world but it put a few quid in my pocket for my university education.

Before I could break away and experience a new life, however, another shock was about to hit me. Helen's cancer had come back and this time with a vengeance.

A few weeks after this news, Dad rang me to tell me that it was terminal and she only had a few weeks left to live. Helen was only in her early forties. I was petrified what this might do to Dad. He didn't recommend that I came down to visit, she had faded fast and was being looked after at home by a team of nurses. She died a few weeks later quietly in bed with Dad and her mother and sisters by her bedside. At least she was free from the pain.

So a couple of weeks before I was to go off to start a new stage of my life at Loughborough, I attended the funeral of my stepmother. I don't handle stress well and the previous 12 months had been the most stressful of my life: an emotional break-up, university interviews, revision, exams, waiting for results, the anxiety of the change that was about to happen and now this. I found that food soothed stress; it was a comfort, a reassurance when things were a bit rocky.

The problem was, whatever my current issue, boredom, if I felt low or was feeling stressed and anxious, I turned to food. It was my rock, my friend, my lover, my counsellor and my support. It was always there for me. When I was weak, it was always dependable. Food was my medicine, my drug, it would never fail to deliver me the high that I sought and over the next 15 years it was going to destroy my life.

Wednesday, 26 November 2008

It's time for my sleep study, some three months after my consultation. The wait has given me time to think about the operation. It's clear to me now that I have no option but to go through with it. My efforts at losing weight have really run out of steam. To be fair, after the first week they never even got properly stoked up. I did manage to cut back a bit on the toast before bed, but everything else just went straight back to normal. As soon as I was tired after work, the takeaway menus came out. I wish Jennie could sometimes cook, it would be really helpful when I don't feel like it. It'll never happen though, so there is no point going on about it.

I need to stay overnight at the hospital while they monitor what is happening when I'm asleep. The TV people are going to be there again, I have to say I've enjoyed the filming for the documentary. It's really positive to be asked some searching questions about my issues. It's really got me thinking. Even after being told I would be dead in five years, I still can't seem to control what goes into my mouth. Why am I so f***ing weak? It really p****s me off. Any other problem or issue in life I've managed to find a solution to. I'd love to have some hypnotherapy to see if they could get to the bottom of it all. If I knew where the problem was or what it was, then that would be the first step in fixing it. But as we aren't able to source the root of the psychological problem, I need a physical solution to the problem. I just hope it won't kill me.

I'm really hoping that I do have sleep apnoea, which I'm sure must sound strange to actually wish you have a medical condition, but it will be comforting to know that's why I'm always falling asleep. Also it means that I'll have more time to get my head round the fact I'm going to have this operation.

The TV people have managed to get me special parking next to the main door. It cuts down on the walking I have to do, which is a real relief. It's terrible going anywhere, I panic about how close I'm going to be able to get my car because I can't walk any distance. It's my first real experience of St Richard's Hospital and I have to say I'm impressed. As I'm doing a sleep study, I'm shown to a private room. It's got a very nice flat-screen telly on the wall, an en-suite bathroom with complimentary toiletries, it's even got nice curtains.

However, I'm in for a bit of a shock. Just as I'm getting comfortable, suddenly I'm bombarded with lots of nurses filling in forms and performing tests on me. I was only expecting to be wired up and settle down to sleep but it appears this is not the case – they are doing a full range of pre-operative tests on me. They ran an ECG – with the sudden stress of what they were doing, I was expecting it to be all over the place, but the good news is that all is completely as it should be. And shock horror! When I get on the scales, which are a bit like a mini weighbridge, I've actually lost a stone! Not much of an achievement in three months, I admit, but at least the scales are going in the right direction. I think that if they had shown an increase I'd have walked out there and then.

Next comes the form filling and again there is an even bigger shock. The first question is 'If it all goes wrong, do you want to be resuscitated?' A bit disconcerting when I think that I was only in for a sleep study! It turns out the question is for the record – I nicely explain that I'm 32, and if they could keep me alive it would be jolly nice, thank you very much. But the question doesn't really build my confidence in the success of the operation.

Come bedtime I'm all wired up to the equipment. How I'm going to sleep with all this crap on I haven't got a clue. I've got a chest monitor, a heart-rate monitor, something going up my nose, an oxygen tester on my finger, a movement indicator running up my arm and then a big recording pack stuck on my stomach. Fortunately, the hospital beds are designed for the task of coping with fat people.

As expected I tossed and turned for most of the night but finally got off around 3.30. Hopefully it will be enough to get results.

I expected to be off at the crack of dawn the next day but they wanted blood and for me to see the consultant anaesthetist. Consequently, I'm sat round for most of the day. I've never been very good at blood tests – they never seem to be able to get any blood out of me. It takes about 15 attempts to finally get the blood. By the end of it, I feel like a tyre with loads of punctures. Then someone else arrives to get blood directly out of my arterial vein – this is to check for the levels of oxygen in my blood. This is a nightmare and the guy hurts me like hell, accidentally catching a tendon on the way through, which sends shock waves up my arm. Next the house doctor returns – some of my blood has congealed before getting to the lab, so we have to go through the same procedure again. I'm delighted!

More waiting around to see this consultant anaesthetist – he sees me at half past three and is with me for five minutes. However, it is a very positive five minutes. He is happy with everything, the ECG and the oxygen levels in my blood, which are more than satisfactory. He is shocked when I tell him I'm on no medication at all. Clearly, most people having this operation are on numerous different drugs. He asks how far I can walk (I say about 100 yards) and then whether I can walk up a flight of stairs (which isn't a problem). I ask what concerns he has and he tells me none, it is a routine practice to do operations on people of my size, and that, after all, it is the reason behind having the operation in the first place. I express concern at my weight and he tells me that actually the weight of a person has no effect on the amount of anaesthetic administered – problems arise due to fitness levels and medical conditions. As I don't have any conditions at present and I'm sure I'm more active than a lot of people who have the operation, I shouldn't have any problems. Many people who weigh as much as I do are relegated to their sofa or, in a lot of cases, are actually bed bound. At least I get up and potter about the house and go to work every day.

I should get the results of the sleep study in a week or so – if I have the condition it's going to be at least three months before the operation; if I don't, then I might be going in for my operation before Christmas and bang will go my last proper Christmas dinner.

I come out of the hospital – finally – really buoyed up and positive, the first time that I have felt like this. This might just work out the way I hope!

6

UNIVERSITY

Leaving home for the first time is a monumental event in anyone's life. For me it was an exciting time, but coupled with that there was also a certain degree of anxiety as I ventured into the unknown. I was going to study Aeronautical Engineering – perhaps a throwback to my spitfire duvet cover days. I had elected to go into halls of residence for my first year, so I wouldn't have the worry of having to cook and look after myself. On the allotted day, I packed my belongings into my car and off I went with Mum and Pete to Loughborough.

I chose Loughborough as it was a campus-based university with an unrivalled reputation for my course. It was also far enough away from home to feel like I had left but not far enough away that I couldn't pop home every other weekend to get my washing done.

We arrived at campus and found our way to Telford

Hall, which was going to be my home for the next 12 months. The hall was a series of blocks arranged around a large grassy quad. I was to be living in Block Eight on the third floor. The accommodation was perhaps best described as basic, although *Bleak House* might be a fairer description. The uncarpeted 8ft by 8ft room had a single bed that was built into the wall, a fitted wardrobe, chest of drawers and a large strip of wood across one whole side of the room which served as a desk area. There was just about enough room for a plastic chair and one armchair. The corridor also had shared bathroom facilities. To say it wasn't the most welcoming of atmospheres would be an understatement.

Normally a shy person, I really made the effort to introduce myself to the rest of the guys on my floor. It was an interesting mix of characters; everyone was studying something different and came from different backgrounds. We all went up to the dining hall for our first meal, for which formal dress was required and we were served an excellent roast chicken dinner. There then followed a series of extremely late nights as we generally got ourselves immersed in university life.

My course started some four days later. I had quite a hectic timetable for a university education. We studied a wide range of subjects including aerodynamics, electrics, fluid mechanics, thermodynamics, design, drawing and mathematics. Normally a lecturer talked to a large group of students and we made notes, a very different method of teaching compared to school. Lectures would normally take place in mornings and then after lunch there would be practical sessions, experiments, computer programming and manufacturing exercises or tutorials with smaller groups. I personally found the university style of education difficult to adjust to. I can see how this method works for humanities subjects but for engineering and mathematical-based areas I really don't think it works well. Of course, I soon realised that there was no register being taken, which meant no one would miss me if I wasn't there. So I started to miss a lot of lectures. Of course, with hindsight, this might not have been the greatest idea I've ever had.

I thought that this practice wouldn't be a problem. Everyone bought a pack of notes at the start of the year, so I had those. Quite frankly, the majority of my lecturers were as boring as hell, even though they may well have been academic geniuses. In all honesty, I was finding the bulk of the course terribly dull; large chunks of it were just passing me by and I found anything more enjoyable than going to lectures. Of course, food was never far from my mind. I'd miss lectures to get back to the block to go to lunch with the guys from the halls and miss afternoon sessions to ensure I got to tea on time. I'd get up in the morning and the first thing on my mind was breakfast. After that my major concern was when everyone else was going to have lunch and then my thoughts would turn to what would be on the teatime menu. In short, my principal driving factor wasn't to get educated, have fun or even get laid – no, my main concern in life was to ensure I'd get fed. If there was a danger that I would miss out on going to a meal with my mates from the block, I would panic and would worry about it until the problem was solved (which invariably meant when I was fed). Of course, at the time, I didn't really see it that way; it is only in retrospect that I can see the damage I was doing.

The kind of food being served in halls didn't really help my weight issues. Firstly there was a cooked breakfast available in the morning. Although it wasn't a 'full' English, I would still knock back two sausages and baked beans every morning. The main item that was available in limitless quantities was toast. I've always loved toast, eaten with loads of thickly spread butter, and here at university it was real butter as opposed to low-fat spread. I would often find myself eating four slices of bread in addition to the cooked breakfast every single morning. Lunches and teas were very similar – a choice of three main courses with potatoes together with some vegetables. Unfortunately, the majority of main courses were cooked in fat and I never ever saw a normal boiled potato in the entire year. The potatoes were served either as chips, sautéed or creamy mash. Vegetables would be simply frozen stuff that had been heated up a long time before serving, so hardly packed with nutrients. There was then a range of sweets to choose from or a piece of fruit. Again, there was limitless bread to accompany every meal. Occasionally, I would have a salad. Salads were always available and I really like them, but the rest of the guys never, ever ate them and at that age it was easy to fall into the trap of doing whatever everyone else does.

Matching other people was also something that I started to do. Everyone knows certain people who can eat like horses and not put on a pound of excess weight. I lived with 12 young men, and there were plenty of this type among us. Some of my friends would eat massive portions of food and of course I found myself keeping up with them. Another guy called Neil lived in the room opposite mine. The guys started calling him 'Little Neil' and me 'Big Neil' to differentiate between us. It came to be expected that I would live up to my nickname: if we went out somewhere, I would have to order the biggest steak, or if we got a burger or kebab after a night on the lash then 'Big Neil' would have to ask what the biggest thing was on the menu.

Alcohol also became a big issue. Before going to university, I never really drank in any great quantity, always preferring the sugary goodness of fizzy pop. But of course at university that all changed. I was pretty good during the first term, but finally succumbed to the dreaded drink about two weeks before we broke up for Christmas. Drinking quickly became a way of life – I was not alone in this by any means, as students the world over spend their three or four years in a drunken stupor. The university campus had no shortage of bars and at least four nights a week we would hit them and hit them hard.

Our favourite bar was the EHB, a short walk from our halls. It was pretty good as there was an abundance of seats, a wide bar area with lots of staff so you didn't have to wait half an hour or so to be served, plus it showed the football! The first night we went, I was greeted by the barman who immediately took me to his bosom as a lifelong friend. Over the course of the next three years, he would relate various humorous stories about rugby and cricket tours we had been on and my 'exploits' on these trips. I found this hilarious, especially as I egged him on – I didn't have the heart to tell him that he had got me completely mixed up with some other poor sod!

The big night out, however, was on a Friday. The huge student union building hosted the originally titled 'Friday Night Disco' or FND. Somewhere in the region of 2,000 very drunk students would frequent this event every single week. The build-up would begin on the Friday afternoon with a trip to Tesco. Students aren't the most well-off people in the world so the idea was to go to the supermarket and buy a pack of beer each to drink before attending FND. Of course, I also took the opportunity when at Tesco to stock up on numerous snacks for the week ahead: crisps, biscuits and chocolate were all piled high into the trolley and to be fair they probably didn't manage to see out most weekends. Then, after tea, we would all pile into someone's room and drink our beers while we watched whatever the current entertainment was – *TFI Friday*, *Top of the Pops* and *The Muppet Show* were all first-rate choices. By the time we were ready to go out at ten o'clock, a good number of cans of lager had already been consumed, with anyone falling behind the required drinking rate severely chastised. We would all nip back to our rooms to put on our best 'pulling' shirts and off we would go.

Of course, very few of us actually did any pulling. Loughborough was a sports- and engineering-dominated university so the number of female students was limited. It was even more limited when you looked like I did. With half of the young sport elite of the UK attending Loughborough, I really had no chance whatsoever.

The one plus point in trying to keep the weight off was that, whenever you wanted to go somewhere around campus, you had to walk. However, by the end of the third term, even this was becoming a problem. Due to the poor food, increased portion size and the drinking, I guess I must have put on a good couple of stone in that first year, the result being that my fitness levels took quite a beating. So much so that, by the time it came to my third term, I found walking very tiring and became increasingly lethargic. This meant that I missed any lectures that were a fair walk away, spending the time on my bed reading instead. Consequently, my examination results were not what might be described as impressive, though I did do enough to ensure that I was able to return for my second year.

I found the long summer months of my first university vacation particularly difficult emotionally, as I tried to come to terms with the previous year. I had the idea of swapping course, something that a number of my friends did, perhaps to study geography. This had always been a subject I had excelled in, but my heart told me that there might be limited opportunities for geographers and the last thing I wanted was to become a teacher. I also felt guilty about changing courses. If I changed, it would have meant that my parents would have had to help support me for another year, something I didn't feel comfortable with. So I decided to stick it out and ensure that I knuckled down in the second year. I didn't want to repeat that stressful feeling of waiting to see the exam results go up and not knowing if I would make the grade or not. I vowed to attend all my lectures the following year.

Living at home for three months helped to prevent my weight running out of control. At last I managed to get a meal with a normal boiled spud! I actually found myself craving healthy food after all the crap that had been served up in the preceding months. The volume of food I ate back home was also reduced, no more cooked breakfasts and no late-night pizzas or burgers from the fast-food joint over the road. I was also playing bowls again, but it was obvious just how out of shape I had become when the guy I was playing with asked if I was OK because my breathing was so bad during one game. It was even more of a concern because the bloke had had three heart attacks, a triple bypass operation and was smoking like a trooper, yet he was worried that I was about to expire! The bowls fortunately got me walking again which meant I managed to regain some degree of fitness.

Summer also meant that I had to get a job. The previous year I had spent time packing up beer, not the most thrilling of jobs to say the least. This year I got a job taking down shelving at the British Transport Depot in Branston, which was the old Branston Pickle factory which had since been converted into stores for all kinds of things. The entire Green Goddess fire engine fleet was stored there before it was sold off to various African fire forces. Also situated there were the Home Office and prison records. As the entire site was being closed and sold off, the records needed to be moved to a new location near London, and somebody had to do it. The warehouse was the biggest thing I have seen in my life, it seemed to stretch for miles and miles. By the time I started my summer job, there were just two areas of shelving and files remaining inside. An outside contractor had been hired to complete the job and he had employed six local lads to provide the labour. The other lads on the job were people that I knew from school, so there was quite a good bit of banter flying around. The job required placing the files, in the correct order, into storage crates, stacking the crates on pallets for transportation and then unscrewing the shelving stacking system. My first week was hell! Pure, unbridled hell! The sweat coming off me created a river running down the warehouse. The first night I got home, I had tea, had a shower and virtually crawled into bed. By halfway through the second week, the contractor had another job to go to, so he appointed one of the guys as 'foreman' and basically we were left to get on with it. This was fortunate – I don't think I would have been able to last much longer at the pace we were cracking on at. Left to our own devices, we soon released that we only had a certain amount of shelving to shift and a whole summer before we went back to university, therefore we adjusted our work rate accordingly. Soon we were extending morning and afternoon break times to half an hour and at lunchtimes we would either play football or cricket in the vast arena that was the warehouse. In the end it turned out to be a great job and we did manage to spin it out all summer. Being a business owner now, I feel guilty about how we took this contractor for a ride, but when you're 19 you don't really feel that way. We had a great time and earned a bit of cash in the process.

During this job, I had a bit of an accident. Quite frankly, the environment was a health and safety nightmare that simply would not have been allowed today. Cries of 'timber' round the warehouse as 20ft-long rows of 10ft-high shelving systems were pushed to the floor for dismantling. There were no such things as steel toe-capped boots or hard hats – we turned up in shorts and T-shirts and just got on with it. We would clamber up the racking to loosen nuts and then remove the sheets of metal between the shelves. The long rows were made up of numerous sections of racking bolted together. At these joins, a sheet of metal was slid in to provide some kind of structural integrity. We needed to remove these sheets before the unit was pushed over, otherwise we might have been left with a nasty injury. However, I wasn't listening properly one afternoon and I forgot to catch the metal sheeting which instead bounced off my chest, creating a bit of a wound. The other guys leaped in to give first aid, but their efforts were hampered when I wouldn't let them pull up the T-shirt because of my awful stretch marks. I nipped down to A&E and got the thing cleaned and stitched up and all was well again. However, if my head had been another two inches closer to the racking, then I could have suffered a very different outcome.

Christmas Day 2008

Happy Christmas! Well sort of, anyway. I know I keep moaning that I want to put the operation off, but really, in the back of my mind, I kind of hoped it would all be done and finished with by Christmas. Then I could look forward to the New Year and a brand-new start. I can't stand all this worrying and waiting. But as it's Christmas I'm determined to be positive – for today at least.

There is one big positive that I can focus on at the moment which is that the continuous positive airway pressure (CPAP) machine seems to be working. I've only had it ten days, I know, and the mask is taking a bit of getting used to, but I think it's helping me to sleep all the way through the night. I haven't been sleeping through the day, so fingers crossed. Last Christmas I was asleep for the whole bloody festive period, so this year it might be nice to actually see some of it.

Amazingly, I did manage to get to a garden centre and buy a Christmas tree last week. Of course, Jennie had to select the six-foot specimen and not go for a shorter one! I had to drive home with the thing sticking out of the window. I even carried it upstairs without having a heart attack. Maybe that stone I've lost does make a difference to my mobility. If a stone makes a bit of difference, then what will happen when five, ten and even twenty come off? Just think, getting rid of 20 stone! I'd like to see it represented visually such as in bags of sugar or something. It's quite unreal if you think about it.

When I start cooking Christmas dinner, I realise this is going to be my last one. Not in a morbid way, but next year I won't be able to eat a 'proper' Christmas dinner. Many people hate cooking at Christmas but I quite like it, it makes everything feel all homely and snug. First job is the turkey. Siobhan, my dad's new partner, has bought a fresh one, so I do a bit of tidying up on the plucking front, give it a wash, slap on some butter then cover with bacon. Finally, I wrap a mountain of foil around it and then shove Tommy in the oven. It fits – just. I'm beginning to get warm, a big problem for me – I'm *always bloody hot. I open the kitchen window, a nice freezing-cold blast comes through. Then I peel enough potatoes to feed the British Army and get them on to boil while I prepare the little sausages with bacon – you can't have Christmas without the pigs in blankets. Jennie comes down and wishes me Happy Christmas and looks at what I'm doing. She asks why we are having 50 sausages. I look at the packages: two packets of 25 cocktail sausages. I realise I may have gone over the top. There are only five for dinner, as Dad and Siobhan are coming round to join me, Jennie and Jodie, but no doubt I'll cook enough for ten. Always been a problem of mine, I think everyone eats the same amount as me, which of course they don't, so I always eat all the leftovers as well.*

After we eat, there is a mountain of food left over! I do always get a bigger turkey than we need because I love turkey and could quite easily eat it every single day of the year. It also means that for the next couple of days I don't have to cook as we live off the leftovers, using the meat for things like sandwiches and curries. We also have a trifle and/or Christmas pudding. Jennie made the trifle; she does it every year and to be fair is bloody good at it, so I confess she

*does cook after all. There is plenty of pudding left.
Add this to the tonnes of special-offer chocolates,
nuts and Christmassy snacks, and we won't be going
short this year.*

*Mind you, I don't actually think I've ever gone
short – it would probably have done me no harm
whatsoever. In fact, it would probably have done me
a hell of a lot of good.*

*Looking at all the leftovers, it does make me think
about how much money I must have wasted on food
over the years. If I hadn't spent all that, not only
would I be thin, but I'd be challenging Richard
Branson for a place on the* Sunday Times *Rich List –
well, almost. Seriously, though, it's a valid point. My
takeaways these days cost 25 quid at a bare minimum,
then add in all the junk food and the excess portions
and we must be talking literally thousands and
thousands of pounds. Then you have to factor in the
additional money I have to spend because I'm fat:
clothing – it's made of so much material that it's never
going to be cheap; cars – I've always had to buy the
biggest car on the market just so I can fit in the thing;
holidays – I can't go on a cheap flight because the
seating is so small, so we normally have to drive or go
on cruises.*

As soon as I've had that operation, Branson and Sugar had better watch out!

7

FOOTBALL AND FINALS

I went back to Loughborough determined to do better and to get my head down and crack on. I teamed up with four of the guys from my floor in halls to sort out alternative living arrangements. Unbelievably, we had found a nice house on an estate about two miles from the university. It wasn't like a typical student house, it had doors, it was painted and even had a carpet. There was no sign of vomit on the floor or rats in the garage. Compared to other student digs, it was a veritable palace.

I decided that this year I was going to make an effort and do something that I might be good at and actually enjoy, because it was unlikely I'd find this on my course. I looked to the various clubs and societies on offer. A few of my friends from my course, fellow back-row slackers, played for the university American football team, the Aces. Throughout the previous year, they had been badgering me to join, my obvious size promising to be a great asset for an offensive line position. So I took the plunge and joined. Dressed in pads and helmet I must have looked a formidable sight. I remember running past a child when we came out for a game and he just looked me up and down as if I were the Colossus of Rhodes. Loughborough is renowned for its sporting reputation and this extends even to minority sports such as American football. We employed a professional coach, who in turn had a further four coaches in tow and we trained Wednesdays and Saturdays, with a tactics night on Tuesdays and finally a match on a Sunday – there were no half-measures.

During my first training session, I nearly died. The amount of running for a man of my size was sheer blind stupidity. Unfortunately, for the 'warm-up' everyone did the same thing – which was running, firstly laps around the pitch followed by 20 minutes of sprinting. This meant 20-stone-plus linemen like me doing the same amount of running as an 11-stone wide receiver – it didn't seem to make any sense at all. So I decided I was going to get myself fit, or at least sufficiently fit to be able to run two laps around a football pitch without thinking that my heart was going to explode out of my chest cavity.

I had already joined a gym with one of my housemates. This was a hardcore bodybuilding-type gym but was great for building those muscles ready for the game. Also, I started going out running. There was a very small block near my house that was a very similar distance to twice round a football pitch. So I went running around that and, yes, I nearly died again. Pounding concrete pavements is not the best thing for a man of my size and after about three of these runs I had developed massive pains along the lengths of my shins. Then, because I was trying to avoid putting pressure on my shins, I managed to pull both of my inner thigh muscles. It was terrible, I could barely walk and getting into my car was almost impossible. I used up two tubes of deep heat rub in as many days trying to get myself right for our first match. Somehow I managed it and I walked straight into the starting line-up for our one and only warm-up game before the full season started. Loughborough were the reigning College Bowl champions and a high proportion of our team were actually Great Britain players, so for a British university team we were good. We duly hammered the opposition, Birmingham in this case, which boded well for the rest of the season.

As our education system drives itself increasingly toward the American administration system, Loughborough University followed suit, changing its academic year from terms to semesters. As a consequence there were two distinct halves to the second year, so, with exams in January that actually counted towards my degree, there was no time for slacking off. As usual, I had pretty good intentions, then I realised that aerodynamics seemed beyond me. Well, *I* couldn't understand a bloody word, anyway. So I felt a better use of my time would be to recover from last night's hangover and then go to a lecture that I might actually understand. The problem was that, once again, there weren't many lectures that I did actually understand. This pressure started to build into stress, there was only a few short months till my first exams. Exams that needed to be passed otherwise it was 'on your bike, mate.' I knew then that I should have gone with my initial gut reaction to the course and binned it and swapped to something that I might actually enjoy and more importantly understand. I turned to my rock and support, the one reassuring voice that would still make sense when everything else around me was shrouded in a cloak of bewilderment – I turned to food.

Everyone in the house cooked separately, so it was always a fight for pots and pans in the kitchen. One of the guys in our house was a bodybuilder and another went out for long runs every day, consequently they ate food like it was going out of fashion, but it was always healthy and wholesome. The other two tended to be 'pickers'. They would eat a small amount at mealtimes and then pack in the junk food between meals. Consequently, I picked up both of these traits. I would eat massive portions of food at mealtimes and then also ate the crap in between.

Why did I do this? I don't know. I think I wanted to feel part of something, have something that I could share with the other people, a bond, be part of the same club. These feelings may go back to having grown up without siblings. This was the first time I had lived with people of my own age; it was a new experience and I really wanted to embrace it. This 'bond' that I was trying to form could have been anything; it could have been on an intellectual level or even something as simple as chasing girls together. As my first thoughts always turned to food, my emotional support, it was food that I used to create my bond. It certainly cost me a fortune. I shudder today when I think of the money I have spent on food over the last 15 years. I seemed to be at Tesco buying food virtually every other day. It was crazy. More weight went on and more clothes stopped fitting me. As I piled the weight on, I became more depressed with my situation and again I turned to my trusted support – food. It was a never-ending circle of pain and misery.

I spent the Christmas holidays of my second year revising for the forthcoming examinations, slowly getting more and more stressed as each day passed. The majority of the work was maths-based, and if you couldn't remember an equation or the appropriate method then you were completely and utterly stuffed. When I came to sit my aerodynamics exam, stuffed didn't even come close to describing the horrors that were laid out on the exam paper. You could purchase past examination papers to get a feel for the type of questions the board has asked in previous years. The exam was spilt into eight sections and in each of those sections would be a question on one of two subjects. Surprise surprise! When I sat down in the hall I realised that every single question that I had revised was not on the examination paper. I simply couldn't answer a single question. I scribbled down a few equations and walked out of the exam 20 minutes into a three-hour paper – receiving the grand score of 4 per cent for my efforts. This meant a resit in summer. If I failed to make the grade second time around, I would be packing my bags. Not all my exam results were dire, I did shockingly well in gas turbine engine theory, for example, only four marks shy of an A. The examiner must have got my paper mixed up with someone else's.

Mercifully, the second half of the year seemed to be a little easier and there was no repeat of these problems in the summer exams. All that remained was for me to return during the summer and pass the bloody aerodynamics course. I revised like a trooper using the past papers and example answers as the basis for my work. This time when I sat the exam, the opposite happened. I could answer every single question and I came out with a massive 86 per cent. This was fortunate, it meant that this result was the one that went forward and was part of my degree. It also created a certain amount of discussion amongst the academics in the department, who couldn't understand how I could possibly get up from 4 per cent to 86 per cent. They thought I had done badly on purpose in the first exam in order to be able to sit it again and have longer to revise. I told them I wasn't that clever to have thought about that.

I actually got a decent job in the summer. I took part in the Shell Technology Enterprise Programme and worked for a company called Checo who made pressure washers and degreasing baths. I had to write the technical manuals for the assembly of their products which was quite good fun, certainly better than packing beer or taking down shelves. The only problem was that there was a sandwich van that would come to the office every day. I would eat my lunch mid-morning and then visit the sandwich man in his van at lunchtime, repeating my past mistake of effectively having two lunches in one day. When the opportunity to eat more presented itself, I took it. It was as though I had no control over my actions.

Saturday, 31 January 2009

I'm not going to get away with this for much longer. It's the end of January. I've already done six weeks on the CPAP machine. Mr Somers told me that he'd be able to do the operation after two or three months, so I'm bound to get a letter soon. The CPAP machine is amazing. It doesn't make a noise and you soon get used to having the mask on. From that first day I got the machine I've slept like a tot. Before I used the machine, I had to get up for a pee three or four times a night – now I sleep all the way through. In reality, a lot of the time I didn't actually need to go. Because I was awake, I think my brain was telling me I had woken for a reason – in the absence of anything else, I thought it must have been because I needed the loo. I had been sleeping all the time during the day. I'd have a sleep for two hours at work and as soon as I got on the sofa at home I'd be asleep again. At weekends I'd get up in the morning just to go to sleep again on the sofa. Of course, none of it was quality sleep. But now that I'm on the CPAP machine I haven't slept once outside of bed at night. It's unbelievable.

I'm nervous waiting for the post to arrive. I dread it every single day. It feels like a death sentence is about to drop through the letterbox. Fortunately, today, I'm saved – nothing in the post but bills and junk mail, and tomorrow is Sunday, so I can relax for another day.

I've gone over every single option to try to think of a way to avoid having to go through with the operation and I've come up with a blank. I was hoping that now I'm sleeping I'll have more energy during the day and will be able to do more. But then I read a report on the Internet that people who are treated with a CPAP machine actually put on weight because they sleep at night and aren't tossing or turning. I can't get this weight off any other way – I have to have the operation – simple as that, but why can't people understand that I'm not going to be happy about it?

Fortunately, my mum is away from most of my moaning and negativity and I try very hard to be positive about it all whenever I talk to her. The last thing I want is for her to worry about all this more than she has to. Dad, however, picks up on the smallest thing I say. He now seems convinced that I'm not going to have the operation. I know I've been down and keeping asking Jennie if it's all going to be all right, but I've never ever said that I'm not going to have the operation. Dad is so convinced that I'm not going to have it done that he's sat down with Jennie to ask her how they should go about getting me sectioned under the Mental Health Act! OK, some people might think I'm insane to get myself into this state, but I don't think it's enough to get me sectioned.

His other master stroke is to give me sleeping pills, tie me up, put me in a van and drive me down to the hospital to get the operation done. Straight up – it was offered as a suggestion in case I decided not to have the operation. I don't know who he was planning to sign the consent forms.

Jennie finally cracks when I go on about the operation yet again this afternoon. She shouts and tells me not to have it done then and continue living the shit life that we have at the moment. I respond with the not-so-clever comment that I'll have it done and then I'll be dead and she'll be happy then and can live the life she wants. Jennie is probably feeling just as bad as me or maybe even worse, as there is nothing she can do to help me. Taking it all out on her isn't going to help either of us. I grovel for forgiveness, a request which seems to be accepted. I make a mental note that I can't

> *keep treating her as a sounding board for all my woes.*
>
> *I need to get my own head round all this. There is no one else who can do this for me. After the operation is done, I'll sit back and think what the hell was I worried about.*
>
> *With luck!*

My final year at university was a year of pure stress. Fortunately, the number of lectures had fallen off and now things were heavily project-based. Me and my housemates had moved back into halls. It was easier than having to worry about cooking and cleaning for yourself. This time, my room was bang opposite the campus shop and fast-food take-out. As the work piled up, so did the Coke bottles, chocolate wrappers and pizza boxes! I had given up the American football, as there was no way I was going to be able to cope with playing and getting through my degree. This meant I had given up the chance to play for Great Britain, as all starters for the Aces were invited to go to the trials. I felt it was more important to get the degree under my belt than a fancy T-shirt with Great Britain on the back.

My biggest problem was my final-year project, titled 'The Evolution of Civil Aircraft Design Criteria'. The project was supervised by one of the older lecturers in the department and, boy, did he give me a hard time. Finally, after about six weeks of meetings and criticism, I finally understood what he was looking for and then had to spend a good month in the library researching the information – anyone would have thought that I was in university to learn! As the year went by and the deadline date drew ever closer, I began to have nightmares about not getting it done in time. Eventually, I completed it and could finally relax. I still get the same nightmares today – I wake up in a hot sweat panicking that I still have another 30,000 words to write, then I realise that university was years ago.

There were so many nights when I had to pull an all-nighter to get my work completed. I remember staying up all night to draw the final design of my jet engine for my gas turbine design project. Everyone can rest safe in their beds knowing that it never made it anywhere near a production line.

The final-year exams came and went, and then I had the stress of waiting for the results. The rest of my friends were all planning on returning for the end-of-year ball but I made the excuse that I was going to be on holiday, which was a lie. The dress code for the event was formal and there was no way I was going to be able to get a dinner jacket to fit me, so I passed without creating an issue out of it. I slipped out of university pretty much as I arrived; I packed up my car and left without fanfare.

My poor little car was really getting battered, as it simply wasn't up to handling my weight. The back of my driving seat had pretty much collapsed and I was propping it up with my spare tyre. Finally it gave out completely. When I checked the screws attaching the seat to the floor of the car, I saw they had simply sheered straight off because of the weight it was carrying. I needed a new car.

Having carefully calculated my coursework grades and previous results, I knew that I was on the border between a third class and a 2.2, otherwise known at the time as a Desmond. A 2.2 would be a respectable result, a third would have been a disaster and would have hampered my future job prospects enormously. As the grades were to be released during the holidays, students had to ring up to receive them. The results should have been out at 10am but at 3.30pm on the allotted day they still weren't available. Then at around 4.30pm they were finally available. It was such a feeling of relief to hear the phase 'Second Class Honours: Lower Division' I could have wept.

So what did I gain from my university experience other than a degree? A handful of decent friends, maybe. But I didn't get that buzz that I was expecting. I didn't get a girl, not even once. I didn't get high on drugs (maybe not a bad thing). What I did get was a whole lot of stress, a mass of debt and a fair few stone around the middle. I also matured and developed habits, emotional tie-ins and associations with food that I would live with for a long, long time.

But things were going to be all right – I was going build a career and take on the world.

8
EARLY CAREER

When it came to looking at the job market, I had only one thing in my mind: there was no was on way on earth that I wanted to have anything whatsoever to do with aeronautical engineering. So that left my net very open and I began the search for something to excite and captivate my interest.

I had in the back of my mind that I might be interested in sales. During my brief spell at Checo the previous summer, I had spent two days knocking on doors in an industrial estate promoting their products. I found it quite a buzz when people showed an interest in what I was offering. I found it easy to relate to people, despite my confidence issues stemming from my weight and the remnants of my stutter. This ability would be a great benefit when it came to sales. The other obvious route it opened up was management. If I could relate well to people, then maybe I would be a good manager. So I also started looking at some of the management schemes that some of the big companies had available.

While I searched for gainful employment, I went back to Checo to do a bit of freelance sales work on their behalf. This involved driving around in my less than tip-top Metro, knocking on doors and attempting to sell degreasing baths and pressure washers. Again, I found the whole experience very exciting. I liked the thrill of getting through the fearsome receptionists and to pitch to the business owners and then when I actually sold something I felt like I was walking on air. But, as good as these feelings were, they didn't compete with the joy I felt at having sandwich vans on every industrial estate I visited: bacon sarnies, sausage sticks and greasy burgers were all available at any time of the day. Most of the money I made in commission went on feeding my face.

All the time I was doing this, I was also looking at the national papers and seeing if anything leaped out and grabbed me. Amazingly, something did look pretty good, despite the name of the company – McDonald's! Now, you don't normally go through three years of hell at university to get a job working at McDonald's. However, they were advertising for graduates for their fast-track management-trainee programme. It was a good starting salary so I thought, What the hell? and applied. It was a long, rigorous process; I had an interview, then another interview and finally was put on a two-day assessment. The assessment was held in-store and run by one of their area managers. He was 27 and earning £35k a year *and* had a company car, so it all seemed pretty appealing. I did a bit of everything on this scheme – worked with cleaners, made the Big Macs, served customers, manned the Drive Thru, cashed up, made orders and did role plays with the manger. It was all very intense stuff. At the end of it all, I received a letter offering me the position. As with previous jobs of mine, there was a problem connected to food. During your break, you could eat what you wanted from the store. This was going to be an issue; there was no way my body could cope with eating a McDonald's every day. I'd end up putting on a stone in my first month. The other issue was shift work – I had hated doing shift work in the past and really didn't fancy doing that for the rest of my working life. Fortunately, I had also been offered another job.

Envirotech Pump Systems was based in Rugby. They were a division of Weir Pumps, a large Glasgow-based manufacturing company. Envirotech made slurry pumps of one form or another, used to pump substances such as sewage, iron ore and, of all things, chicken feet! The job title was Applications Engineer, basically an internal sales position in which I would handle the incoming enquiries, produce quotations and try to assist the external sales guys. The salary was higher than the McDonald's job and I felt it was a more pleasant environment in which to work.

As the job was based in Rugby, around an hour's drive from my mum's, it meant that I certainly needed a new car. I got a loan and purchased a large 4x4. Big, black and intimidating looking, I thought it was fantastic, until I started driving it and realised how much money it was consuming in petrol. Then I needed a new tyre, and, as they were a little bit bigger than the tyres on the Metro, the price was a fair bit bigger as well. Having to make a lot of petrol stops meant that I was going into a lot of garages, and every day when I drove home I stopped and bought a cheese baguette, crisps, chocolate and Coke. I'd eat them on the rest of the drive home, walk through the door and sit down at the table and eat my dinner.

Eating had now become a habit. When I did certain things – whether pleasurable or not – I would relate them to eating. When I drove home, I would have to stop and buy food. It was the most important thing that had been on my mind since I had finished eating lunch. One summer evening, it was extremely hot and when I got home and started to eat tea, which was a big cooked meal, I felt terribly unwell, all dizzy and nauseous. I had to go and sit outside to try to cool down. I blamed the heat but I knew the real reason for this hot flush was because I had eaten too much on the way home. As usual, I resolved to break this destructive cycle, as it was obviously doing my health no good as well as badly hurting my pocket – a fiver a day on additional snacks you don't need soon adds up. So I climbed in the car determined not to make any stops or eat on the way home. As I approached the garage, I began to feel very odd, I was twitchy, nervous and began to feel sick. Then I broke out in a cold, clammy sweat. I drove past the garage and I literally started to shake. It was no good. I physically had to stop and buy food. I quickly turned the car round and pulled in. Were these the first signs of addiction? Did I need my daily high, my fix? The answer, simply, was yes. I was fast turning into a food junkie!

For people who haven't experienced this feeling, it must be very difficult to understand. The obese are often looked upon as being greedy and lazy. People who aren't in this situation typically say, 'Stop eating and do more exercise!' but unfortunately it isn't as simple as that. My dependence on food was becoming more and more acute. It is only in retrospect that I realise that the physical symptoms are a sign of this emotional dependence. I now recognise that this was the stage when I should have sought professional help, but dependency on anything, especially food, is considered a weakness in our society. So, like many others who are dependent on drink, drugs or cigarettes, I refused to admit to myself that I had a problem and I carried on in the same destructive manner.

The issues with the food aside, my first job was all right, but nothing more. It wasn't as thrilling as I had first imagined. The company employed a lot of people much older than me, so, as the new boy starting out in the world of work, at first it was a bit of a surprise that my expectations and the reality of the nine-to-five were somewhat out of synch. However, there were two guys similar in age to me and they introduced me to the concept of visiting the pub at lunchtime. Every Friday we'd go to the local boozer and knock back two pints and a burger and chips. When the local Harvester began to do a pint and lunch for a fiver, we were really in trouble and spent every lunchtime for a fortnight in there. These guys were OK but I felt they weren't quite on my level, the only topics for discussion being birds and football. Some may ask, what else is there in life at 21? But I was always searching for something more and, when one of my university mates said he was applying for a job in Maidenhead, it spurred me on to start looking at the job market again.

I got in contact with a specialist recruitment agent who specifically worked in the pump sector. He said there was a large American firm called Flowserve based in Esher, Surrey, that was looking for a Regional Parts Specialist.

The job was selling the spare parts for their large oil-refinery pumps, the majority of which were based in the Middle East. I said I was interested and was offered an interview. It has to be said it was one of the strangest experiences of my life. The principal interviewer called another colleague over, as there was another job going in a different department. This guy was a fellow man of 'girth' who immediately expressed his delight at how it was very clear that I enjoyed my food. I accepted the offer of a second interview.

The second interview was held in the firm's Milton Keynes office as it was less far for me to travel. This was a more formal affair, held with the Esher office sales manager. I was offered the job on the spot. The salary was good, a big hike on my previous figure, I would be on a bonus scheme and even more impressively would go to the annual sales meetings. The previous year's had been held in Long Beach, California – so, without much hesitation, I accepted.

The management at Envirotech were shocked when I handed in my notice. They said I was progressing well and had a good future with the company. In fact, they tried everything to keep me, even offering me the Scandinavian and East European sales position when the current incumbent retired the following year, which would have been an impressive promotion for someone only recently out of university. But my mind was made up, the clincher being able to leave home again and live with one of my university friends.

We found a small maisonette in Reading. This was some way away from the office in Esher, but as renting housing in that part of Surrey is about as expensive as trying to purchase the crown jewels, it was the closest that I could get (they don't call it the stockbroker belt for nothing!). This again left me with an hour's drive to and from work each day. I of course wasted no time in filling the wasted hour on the way home with the essential task of eating.

The job itself turned out to be fantastic for this 22-year-old. Principally, the position was the management of the spare-parts sales for pumps in the UK, South Africa and the holiday hotspots of Iran, Iraq and Libya – business worth around $20m annually. On my very first day, I signed a quotation for spare parts totalling $235,000. It was a bit different from quoting pumps at £2,000! Of course, on my first day, a welcome session was held in the pub which was a mere 20 yards away from the office door. The Albert Arms in Esher was a fantastic place, the regular haunt of snooker legend Jimmy White. It was a spit-and-sawdust type of bar, but come Friday afternoon it was choc-a-block, a real gold mine. Whereas at Envirotech it was just the young chaps that went down the pub, here everyone went and on a regular basis. So much of the business was conducted in the bar that there would regularly be suppliers in to buy the whole office lunch, or we would be off the premises, buying lunch for our customers. This was all part of the culture and something that you really couldn't abstain from, despite the negative effects on the waistline.

Then there were the trips overseas. I'd been at the company only a month and in that time had visited the main factory in Etten-Leur in the Netherlands twice. I had spent as much time overseas as I had in the office. These trips were fantastic: during the day you would get a lot of work done and get to know people who you would speak to on the phone on an almost hourly basis when back in the UK. Then, during the evening, it would be a meal and a long piss-up into the night. Much of the beer in Holland comes from its quiet neighbour Belgium. The beer of choice in the Etten-Leur area was Palm, a lovely creamy brew served in an outsized brandy glass. Many of these were served to us during the course of an evening.

My second business trip was spent with our Iranian agent. To operate in all Middle Eastern countries, Western firms either had to have agents or 'sponsors'. The agents would smooth the waters and make business happen 'quickly', and would receive a percentage of the sale for their not inconsiderable trouble. 'Quickly' in Iran is slightly different from my own definition of the word. The way it worked was that I would provide the agent with a quotation, they'd argue about it with various 'intelligent' questions and then nine or ten months afterwards an order would be placed. The process wasn't over then, though, as receiving an order was really only the start of the process. Next, we had to be sure that we would get our money. As every single part of each pump was completely unique, we couldn't risk starting to manufacture the parts until we knew that we would be paid – a feeling of mutual trust didn't exactly flow between the parties involved. They, quite understandably, didn't trust us either. This is where a letter of credit came into play. Basically, the client paid the money into a 'neutral' bank and, when the bank was given the appropriate documents to say the parts had been received in Iran, the bank would give us the money! A brilliantly simple system that enables businesses to function the world over.

Back to the matter of our trip with the Iranian agent. For some reason I was expecting a very sober week. Not the case! Beer, wine and whiskey were all consumed in equal measures while I was there. I still remember a classic night on the Hoegaarden beer, eating frogs' legs and then me and the Iranian guy hammering the locals at pool!

My life was like that of any typical young man living with his friends. Appalling, unhealthy food, quite often a takeaway or a burger down the pub watching the football, lots of beer and late nights. I went through a period of realising that I had already had a cooked dinner at lunchtime down the Albert so really should only have a sandwich at night. Unfortunately, that 'sandwich' turned into a whole French stick, with thickly spread butter and half a pound of cheese, accompanied by lashings of coleslaw and crisps – far better for me than a hot meal!

We would always have a big night out on a Friday and would continue our university practice of getting completely lashed before going out. I was a bit of a marketing man's dream when it came to buying alcohol in the supermarket. Companies would often give away glasses or can dispensers with their 12-packs, free goodies which I keenly snapped up. I often bought strange bottles of spirits – Rebel Yell, an American whiskey, was a particular favourite at university. This was often consumed in great quantities to loud cries of 'Rebel Yell!' at the end of an evening. On my trips to Holland, in addition to purchasing a crate-load of Palm to take home, I had also discovered an interesting-looking schnapps drink with a skull and crossbones on the label. Clearly, this should have been a warning sign – but boys will be boys! It went in the freezer to chill to a suitable temperature and, on my first Friday back, out came the bottle. The whole lot was consumed in front of the telly. My flatmate was not yet home so I started knocking the booze back heavily. When he got home I was firmly lubricated and in fine voice (in those days when I got drunk I was always extremely loud!). Off we went into Reading, deciding to kick off the weekend in the Firkin pub, with me ensuring everyone in earshot that it was going to be a great night. The first pint went down fine and we ordered a second. Then I managed to fall asleep on the bar. The security guys came in to 'enquire' as to my health and my friend tried to wake me by rubbing his knuckles hard across the back of my skull – I didn't even flinch. 'It was then that I knew we were in trouble,' my friend has since said! Somehow I was stirred from my slumber and taken outside to gets some air. However, I managed to place the contents of my stomach all over the stairs to the pub, much to the disgust of the staff and the queue of people waiting to come in. I was bundled into a taxi and my friend took me home, it was 8.15pm! Not really the great night I was expecting.

However, what didn't feature in my nights out were young ladies. The fact that I was fat meant that I simply had no confidence to approach anyone and they certainly weren't approaching me, although one or two young men did show an occasional interest. For five years I had had no encounters with ladies and this became a source of great amusement in the office, which, of course, only succeeded in damaging my confidence even more. They even went as far as saying that, next time I went to Holland, they would have a whip-round so I could go and visit one of the legal establishments there. I was getting so desperate I'd probably have done it, but in the end they were all too tight-fisted. I then became convinced that a girl who worked at the local bank fancied me. She was clearly a few years older than me, not that that mattered, and she would always greet me with a friendly hello and have a little chat. I didn't even know her name so she became known as the 'Bank babe'. One or two guys from the office tried to point out that, being a cashier in a bank, it was her job to be friendly, so a simple 'Hello' and 'How are you today?' didn't really mean that she wanted me! But I would be in there every single day; there was no one in Esher who was doing more banking than me! Of course, I never had the courage to get it all over and done with and actually ask her out! Fortunately, she eventually put me out of my misery, probably fed up after printing out my 200th statement in the last three months, by casually mentioning that she was going away on holiday with her boyfriend the following week. I was gutted!

An office job meant a real lack of exercise, so me and my flatmate joined the local gym. In the introductory session, they conducted a body-fat percentage test and interestingly they found that my lean body mass, just muscle, bone and internal organs, was 17.5 stone. It was clear that I was never going to be small! It was then that I started a cycle of yo-yo dieting. My lifestyle was clearly having a seriously detrimental effect, especially when the office went through a period of sending someone out for bacon butties mid-morning. I was actually eating five meals a day! Breakfast before leaving the maisonette, my greasy bacon sandwich, a lunch down the pub with a couple of beers, the compulsory sandwich, crisps and choccy on the way home and then invariably a none-too-wholesome dinner at night! Sometimes there would even be little snacks between and a few crisps in front of the telly once I was back home. When someone at the office said that there was no real need for me to eat every hour, I began to realise the amount I was actually shovelling away. So I really made an effort to get things under control. I could see my life turning into a constant state of bachelorhood and loneliness. My efforts started well, at least for a fortnight or so, giving up the pub at lunchtime and having a turkey salad roll instead. I even managed to drive past the garage without stopping, which I felt was an amazing achievement. During that time, I would clearly lose weight. How much I lost I wouldn't know, as I'd long outgrown the bathroom scales. I would feel better in myself, my clothing would be looser, I'd have more energy and feel more alive. But something always drove me back to my bad habits. Food had become the major part of my life; it was impossible to break my bond with it. It was like a seductive mistress in the corner, beckoning me over to sample her many delights. When I did fall off the wagon, I would fall heavily and more weight would go on than I had lost, and always in such a short period of time. The never-ending circle of despair would then show its face, I would be shocked and depressed at my latest failure, which would spark another round of excessive consumption to make me feel better.

Despite my confidence issues with women and my own self-loathing at my weaknesses when it came to controlling my demons, the one area about which I had little self-doubt was work. I was convinced I was going to become the youngest-ever CEO of the company. My sales figures were always impressive with the Iranians and Libyans having to spend millions to ensure that their oil infrastructure was maintained. We were also starting to get orders from Iraq. This was between the Gulf Wars when they had to do all their business via the UN Oil for Food Programme. We'd get three or four orders a year, each for over $1 million. All the wheels were kept turning in a suitable manner by our agent based in London, who would regularly make trips over to Jordan and then 'pop' over the border via a desert route. The official orders would all come in the post, on massively high-quality paper, with an embossed government crest on the top and the words Iraqi Ministry of Oil emblazoned across them. They were signed by the Minister of Oil, a guy called Saddam Hussein (yes, Hussein!) – I wish I kept one or two for framing in my downstairs cloakroom. These weren't the only unusual communications I would get on a regular basis. Messages from Iran would come out of the fax machine on a daily basis and always at the top of each one would be typed 'IN THE NAME OF GOD' – it was like having a direct link straight to heaven! When I first joined, I was confused by the addresses on some of the documents I got from Libya. The address would say something like, 2353 Swanee Road, Tripoli, GSPLAJ. Putting aside why a road in Tripoli was named after an Al Jolson song, what was GSPLAJ? This was a term often used in the office, 'Have you heard anything from GSPLAJ?' or 'What's going on in GSPLAJ?' I finally had to ask, 'What is this GSPLAJ?' It appears that Libya isn't actually its official name. Outside of the country, everyone simply calls it Libya, but inside the official name given to it by Gaddafi after his coup in 1969 is used. GSPLAJ actually stands for Great Socialist People's Libyan Arab Jamahiriya (Jamahiriya meaning 'Paradise' in Arabic) – you learn something new every day. For a 22-year-old, it was an immense experience learning about all these different cultures and beliefs, although with these regular communications I was convinced that one evening I'd be bundled into a blacked-out car by four big men in dark suits and sunglasses and be questioned about why I was getting all these faxes from Iran, Iraq and Libya.

Being classed as a salesman, the Regional Parts Specialist was also invited to the annual sales meeting, which in my first year was to be held in Dallas, Texas. This was my first trip to the States and I was extremely excited. I normally hate flying, strange for a man with an aeronautical engineering degree, but this trip promised to be pretty good fun. It started off well because, instead of being crammed in my seat, the majority of the flight was spent stood at the back of the plane with a handful of the other guys consuming as much beer as we could. The stewardess actually gave up the command of the trolley and one of our number acted as barman for the rest of the flight. This really started the week the way it was going to carry on. They say that 'everything in Texas is bigger', which was certainly true of the quantities of beer and food consumed during our stay there. The steaks were so huge even I couldn't finish one off and, as the beer was on expenses, a constant supply of bottles of lager stood on the bar. There were various team-building sessions in the afternoons, the most bizarre of which was a visit to a large driving complex with various go-karts, simulators and even drag racing. Not very bizarre, you might say, but it was when you were doing it with a bottle of beer in your hand – the first and only time I have ever driven while drinking. However, it wasn't all partying. At seven in the morning, we would be transported for an hour along the roads of Texas to Flowserve University – FU! Here the Regional Parts Specialists for all over Europe had a meeting to discuss strategy. I was particularly vocal in these sessions and, as the youngest employee in Dallas by quite some distance, was easily spotted by the Vice-President of Sales. I was told by my boss that the Vice-President had mentioned me to the CEO of the company as someone to look out for in the future.

When we got back to England, my eating problems continued. I'd start my day with three or four slices of toast, all thickly spread with butter and washed down with a pint of fresh orange juice. The visits to the bacon-sandwich van became a more regular occurrence. If I wasn't down the pub at lunchtime, I'd find the pleasures of a cheese and crispy bacon baguette covered in lashings of calorie-laden mayonnaise. If you add this to the sandwich I was eating on my drive home and toast before bedtime, then I bet I wasn't far off eating a loaf of bread a day! In hindsight, analysing my eating habits, it is interesting to see that most of my vices were savoury. Yes, I did eat chocolate, but I wouldn't eat it in massive amounts in the one blow-out session like I did during my exams. Cake is often something that many fat people make a beeline for, but it wouldn't have bothered me if cake were removed from the face of the earth. The same was true of puddings. The only time I have ever eaten pudding in my whole life is on holiday or when out for a meal – and I didn't go out for meals very often. My craving for sweet stuff was satisfied by the pints and pints of Coke I would drink. I guess I was drinking around eight pints of the sugary nectar each and every day. But my worst sin was the bread, ideally toasted, but it didn't really matter just as long as it was covered in lashings of butter. I call it butter, but it never was, it was 'low-fat spread', which I managed to convince myself was practically a health food, what with having the words 'low-fat' on the packet. I also gorged on crisps. Now I was free from the constraints of living with my parents and was doing the shopping myself, I soon found the large bags of crisps, the ones that you buy for a party or for grabbing one handful from and then leaving the rest until the next day. Of course my bag disappeared during the first half of the football. Other savoury delights that made a regular appearance in my diet included sausage rolls, pork pies and anything with bacon in. As my body was becoming more and more used to the volume of food I was putting in, the more it craved, so much so that I was suffering from a permanent hunger. After an hour or so without eating, I'd be getting jumpy thinking about where my next snack or meal was coming from. My weight had got so bad that work even got me a special larger chair in order to accommodate me. It was no way to live my life. I don't know exactly how much I weighed at this time – all I know is, I was too heavy even to stand on a regular set of scales.

After about six months of living together, me and my flatmate decided to move in with two other guys from university. We got a bigger, detached house, this time a little closer to work. It was here, after getting another nightclub brush-off from a girl, that I made a massive push to shed some pounds. I picked up playing squash again. Although I got hammered every single match, I was at least doing some exercise. I also started playing golf. The word had got round that quite a few of the guys in the office played nine holes after work in the summer. Golf wasn't too taxing on the body and as many businessmen played the game it made it an ideal skill to add to my CV, although skill wasn't exactly the word that was used regularly with my golf game. I'd measure my success on a round by how many balls I had lost! As a former crown green bowler, I thought I would be good at putting, but it turned out that I had a touch like a bull elephant and often took more shots on the green than I did getting the ball to the green. As appalling as my golf and squash were, at least I was doing some exercise and not sat in the pub or in front of the box every night. When I combined this with my latest regimented eating plan, I did lose some weight.

I made the decision that I had to get a grip on my weight or it would run out of all control. I knew, if I didn't do something, no girl in their right mind would ever be interested in me. I also knew that my suit for work would soon give way under the pressure and I might even outgrow my own special chair. And I knew deep down that, at some point, food was going to kill me. Somehow – and I still don't how I managed it – I gained control of all of my eating addictions. At breakfast I would have two slices of toast. I completely got rid of the butter and just had jam. Then at lunchtime, I would scrap the pub during the week and walk down to the sandwich shop where I would get a turkey salad roll with no dressing. I might even have an apple as well. On a Friday I would still visit the pub with everyone else, but, instead of the normal lager with burger and chips, I had a tuna sandwich and a couple of glasses of lime and soda water.

My biggest problem was beating that old habit of stopping at the garage on the way home, but as I had moved only half an hour's drive away from the office, this became a little easier. I also made sure that when I needed petrol I would get it in the morning, just after I had eaten breakfast, so I had no need to stop on the way home. The other thing I did was to ensure that I knew I was going to eat dinner as soon as I walked through the door. By this stage in the day I was starving! But instead of walking in and grabbing some bread and cheese as I would have done in the past, I got dinner started straight away, therefore resisting the urge to eat crap. I made sure that my meals were quick, easy and that they would be on my plate in a matter of minutes. I alternated between penne pasta, a slice of chopped ham and sugar snap peas all mixed with a tablespoon of a Ragù sauce, and a vegetable stir fry. Then, when I began to feel hungry at night, I simply went to bed – it did make for a hell of a lot of early nights. How I managed to stick to this plan, I simply don't know. If I knew the answer, then I'd never have got myself back into the position I found myself in and I'm sure I'd be a very rich man.

For around six wonderful months, I broke the shackles of having to consume. I wouldn't say I had beaten food, because my every waking thought was about it (sometimes I would even dream about it). It was really hard going especially at weekends, but I stuck to it. My routine was the same, day in, day out: it was hideously monotonous. But it had to be. I had to know what I was eating and when, I had to lose that freedom of choice. With everything planned out I knew what I was eating and therefore there was no room to transgress. I also ditched the high-calorie drinks. I tried to stick to water wherever possible but, when the desire for the black stuff came, I made sure it was the diet variety. During those six months, the weight came off and came off quickly. I reclaimed my suit, my jeans and all manner of clothing I hadn't worn for ages. I even managed to buy a sweatshirt from Marks and Spencer, the first time I had bought clothes from a regular shop in years. What's more, I almost made it into a pair of combat trousers, but just missed out on this. The disappointment didn't last long, though. My housemates were all very supportive, saying how well I had done. I expressed my concern that I might put the weight back on, but they told me that, as I had put so much effort in, there was no way I was going to go back to my previous habits.

But, of course, that is exactly what happened.

I was alone in the house for the weekend as everyone else had gone to see their parents. I think it may have been Easter week. I was planning on watching the US Masters on television and I was craving something creamy and fatty so on my way home I pulled in at the off-licence and bought a big bottle of that manly drink Baileys! After that first sip, I was away, lost in my gratification. It was so rich and creamy, it sounds hideous but I could almost feel the fatty goodness going down into my stomach, giving me the pleasure I had been missing for so many months. That night in front of the golf, I drank the full bottle. The next day I did the same thing. I nipped into the off-licence and bought another bottle, this time adding a massive packet of cheddar cheese Kettle Chips. Such was my excitement, it was like I was enjoying an illicit evening with a blonde bombshell. I have to admit to being somewhat disappointed when one of my housemates came home; it was as if I'd been found out and someone was going to tell the wife.

For the next six months, I fought a battle against my desires. Some days I was good and others I was bad, very bad. In many ways I was living a 'normal' lifestyle: one day you go down the pub and have a lager and a bowl of chilli with a huge slice of crusty bread, then the next day you cut back and back sure that you eat a salad and loads of fruit. Certainly, I wasn't indulging in the regular massive excesses of the past, but things like takeaways, crisps and chocolate were creeping back in. Weight crept back on, but it was only creeping. We moved house again later in the year, as one of our housemates decided to go his own way. This time we moved to Wokingham, near Reading. As usual, I had to work over the period between Christmas and New Year – after all, people in the Middle East don't celebrate Christmas. The other guys all had time off and were at home with their families – so I was on my own. It was here, on the eve of the millennium, that I met Jennie.

9

A READY-MADE FAMILY

I used to read about people who had found their future spouses on the Internet and think that they were very, very sad. I never dreamed for a moment that I would turn out to be one of them.

I was working in the 'twilight zone' – that strange period between Christmas and New Year. It was 1999, the eve of a brand-new dawn, a new age, and I was hoping a brand-new future. I didn't really want to come back to a desk bending under the weight of Iranian faxes, so I decided to go into work and not waste my valuable holiday. It was actually quite a good time to work. For those magical three days, you could come in late, have an extended lunch break and then bugger off early. At the same time as the shortened hours, I could deal with all my Middle Eastern correspondence without being constantly interrupted on the phone by

British and South African clients with sudden emergencies. The roads were also quiet, almost spookily so – for the first time in my live I drove at 70mph on the M25. My two housemates had both returned home to be with family during the festive period, so I was on my own in the evenings, with very little to do. I decided, for a laugh and to pass the time, to visit a chatroom. This was the first time I had ever done such a thing. Computers weren't really my scene – I still had my old model from university which just about managed to do modern things like email. I dialled up to connect to the Internet (these were the days before broadband) and soon found myself in a chatroom. After laughing quietly to myself at some of the more bizarre conversations going on in front of my eyes, I thought, What the hell? and signed up. The anonymity of the computer screen offered some protection, as no one knew who I was. The username I chose didn't take a lot of thought – bigfella. After a few short exchanges with a few ladies, someone called Mara Jade started chatting. She, in fact, wasn't the wife of Luke Skywalker but was called Jennie. She said she was 28, so thinking on my feet I quickly claimed to be 26 – after all, it wasn't like we were ever going to meet. At four o'clock in the morning, some six hours later, we were still chatting. It was quite remarkable, we got on like a house on fire, the conversation flowed and it felt so natural. At 4.30 in the morning, I took a big step and asked for her phone number, as I reasoned it could just as easily have been a 50-year-old bloke I was chatting to. With my fancy patter of the previous few hours, I was full of confidence and I rang her there and then. We ended up talking on the phone for another hour, there just seemed to be an instant connection between us.

The brilliant thing about the Internet method of meeting someone is that you can get to know each other without either party seeing what the other looks like. After the phone call, I realised that this smoke screen was just what I needed in order to meet women. The smoke screen meant that my confidence problems about both my weight and my stutter just weren't an issue. Through the magic of the keyboard, I came over as confident and very sociable – everything, in fact, that I wasn't. Even better than all of this, I could stuff my face with crisps, chocolate and fizzy pop while chatting up girls!

The next few nights, I went online and Jennie was there waiting for me, always introducing herself with the line 'Hello Sweetie'. I found out everything about her: she was divorced, had a five-year-old daughter called Jodie, lived in Southend-on-Sea and, having worked as a nurse, was now an area manager for a nursing agency. Such was the connection between us that we agreed to meet in the first week of the new millennium.

I drove down to Southend. Jennie was with one of her friends who was also meeting a bloke she had met on the Internet. Clearly she was being very sensible and making sure that I wasn't a mad axe murderer – however, how did *I* know that she wasn't going to drug me and chain me up in a dungeon somewhere? We met at her friend's flat. I was dressed in my best Johnny Cash combo, a black suit and shirt, black of course being a very slimming colour. Jennie had already sent me a photo. She was quite a big girl and I had already told her that I wasn't going to be the slimmest man she had ever met. Her friend greeted me at the door – Jennie was still getting ready apparently! In fact, she was in the kitchen slugging back vodka and Red Bulls, trying to work up the courage to come and say hello. Eventually, she made it into the lounge. She was wearing a bright lime-green top and she had her blonde hair all over her face, as if she was trying to hide behind it. We got on extremely well, and having had that initial contact over the Internet and not going in face-to-face straight away made all the difference confidence-wise from my point of view. I knew from that first date that this was going to be the start of something special.

We started seeing each other on a regular basis. I'd drive down to Southend from the office and end up staying the night, then getting up early in order to get in to work in time. However, we both had confessions to make and both about the same thing, our ages. I coughed for the fact that I was actually 23, not the 26 that I had led her to believe. Then she told me she was actually 30, which a few dates later changed to being 33! She also let it slip that she wasn't actually divorced as yet, but had started the proceedings. I have to confess I was a little bit shocked – I was dating a woman ten years older than me and the woman was still someone else's wife! I felt like Dustin Hoffman in *The Graduate*. The lack of the divorce certificate didn't bother me in the slightest – if anything, it made it all the more exciting. The age thing did play on my mind, but it really wasn't a concern for her. But then I realised, what did it matter as long as I was happy? Why throw away the chance of happiness for a number on a driving licence?

After our third date, I met Jennie's five-year-old daughter Jodie. Dating a woman with a daughter wasn't something that had ever crossed my mind, but here I was seeing an older woman complete with family. I got on really well with Jodie, and she didn't seem to have a problem with me dating her mother at all. I think she liked having someone else to play with her – teachers was her favourite game! We took her to the park, to the cinema and to Kids Kingdom, a huge warehouse filled with overexcited four- to ten-year-olds and various scramble nets, slides and climbing equipment – it was one hell of an experience.

For the first time in ages, I was contented. I had at last found someone. I was finally enjoying a relationship like any other 23-year-old man, with all that that entails. But feelings of happiness began to give way to complacency. The thing that had driven me to lose weight the previous year, and not to completely fall off the wagon afterwards, was the fact that if I didn't I would likely end up as a fat and lonely bachelor. As I had now found someone, I slipped back into the dreaded routine of eating. I'd even end up ordering pizzas at 11 o'clock at night while I was staying over at Jennie's flat. When I drove home at the end of the weekend, I would always stop off in the Drive Thru McDonald's and load up on lovely carbohydrate and fat. Why was I doing this if I was happy? It was strange, I could understand the fact that I ate when I was sad, I could understand the fact that I ate when I was upset and I could even understand eating when I was bored. But eating when I was happy – why? I think by this stage my entire life had become so intrinsically linked to food that I simply ate all the time. It was part of me, part of my make-up, my very essence of being. I believed that, whatever emotion I was feeling, food would be a welcome addition. It would either be the solution to a problem or, in happier circumstances, enhance my positive feelings.

My new-found love-life did present me with one or two problems. Firstly, I had to go to the doctor as I'd started suffering pains in my abdomen. It was so bad at work one day that I thought I had appendicitis. I have never liked going to the doctor, and my GP at the time needed to work on his bedside manner. I'm sure that if I went to him with my leg hanging off he would simply say, 'What do you expect, Mr Bakewell? You're very overweight.'

Although I say it with a certain amount of humour, this is a very valid point not confined to my local GP surgery – so few of the doctors I have encountered over the years have had the slightest idea on how to go about giving real, constructive advice on losing weight. I still remember my first appointment with this doctor, it was actually quite comical. Nothing at all was the right size for me: the scales only went up to 20 stone, useless for me; I couldn't fit on the bed, it was crammed in against the wall and, being only 6 foot long, it wasn't going to accommodate my 6ft 5in frame. Then the poor man wanted to take my blood pressure and couldn't get a cuff big enough to fit around my bicep. Anyway, after a few pokes and prods, it turned out that my stomach pain wasn't a result of appendicitis, just the overuse of muscles in that area because of my newly acquired sexual prowess.

One night I was forced to save Jennie from the indignity of having to be rescued by the fire service while naked in bed. Jennie had an old-style bed with a big wrought-iron headboard attached to the legs. Unfortunately, the main structure of the bed was made of wooden slats. During a particularly passionate evening, my knee went through one of the slats, then the motion of the bed caused the legs to give way and the headboard to come crashing down, trapping Jennie's head in the process! After Jennie almost turned purple with the pressure, I realised it was my weight causing the problem. Once we'd done some metal bending, Jennie was free. After that, we just put the mattress on the floor!

The second not-so-positive side effect of my new love-life was tiredness. I was used to being in bed at 10pm and getting a good solid eight hours' sleep. Now, however, I was getting into bed earlier, but not necessarily getting the eight hours' sleep. Couple this with all the driving I was doing from Wokingham to Southend and then to Esher and back, and I was shattered. My boss told me he didn't know what was up with me. 'It's like you've got your head in the clouds,' he said.

To be fair on him, it *was* like I had my head clouds – I was in love and was ready to take an even bigger step.

After six months of dating, Jennie and I decided that if our relationship was going to progress further we needed to take the step of moving in together. So we decided to look at an area that was about halfway between our two workplaces. We settled on Sevenoaks. It seemed to be an ideal location, on the M25 with great access to both of our offices. But when we investigated a little further we found that the rental prices were far too expensive on our limited budget. The only places that we managed to see were small cottages and one of them was so small I had to bend down when standing at my full height! So we went a little further outside the M25 and settled on Tonbridge. We found a nice semi-detached house, took the plunge and went for it. It was a shock for my housemates that I was moving out; it all seemed to happen so quickly.

It was a massive change in lifestyle for me, living with a woman and having to be a father figure. When we moved in, Jodie was at her nan's so she didn't get in harm's way or hold us up while we were shifting our belongings. We knew that, as hard as the adjustment was going to be for us, it was going to be a hundred times more difficult for Jodie. She would have to start again at a new school, which at the age of six was never going to be easy. Probably even more major than this change, she also had to adjust to dealing with me being around all the time. To be fair to her, though, she never made any negative comment or expressed any wish that we shouldn't move in together. As some form of compensation for the disruption in her life, we bought her a whole set of new bedroom furniture including one of those bed systems incorporating a desk underneath and a bed on the top, reached by clambering up a ladder. The only problem with this plan was that all the furniture was flat-packed, meaning of course that I would have to assemble it. DIY skills were never my strongest asset, I was at the back of the queue when God was handing them out. I remember building a set of free-standing shelves for my bedroom at university and my friends had to come and take over because of my sheer incompetence. I never seemed to be able to get the hang of power tools, either. I'd create so many holes in the thing as I attempted to put a single screw in. So for this task I went back to the trusted hand-held screwdriver. Over two long 18-hour days, I finally managed to assemble all the bedroom furniture and when I went to sleep my arm was still twisting like I was screwing an imaginary screw into position. Jodie was thrilled with it all, so much so that she was sick down it the very first night. Amazingly, I actually did such a good job that some of the furniture is still standing to this day.

Jennie only had one fault, which I didn't really understand the implications of until we moved in together. At work she was brilliant, all of her staff were behind her and she made things happen; at home she was a doting mother and she clearly adored me. But, unfortunately, she was no domestic goddess. She couldn't or wouldn't cook and had absolutely no interest whatsoever in correcting that chink in her armour. She also had a very strong aversion to food shopping – clothes shopping she could do for hours on end without the need for rest or replenishment, but asking her to go food shopping was like asking her to jump off a cliff. There was no alternative but for me to do both of these tasks. The food shopping wasn't really a problem – it was just a case of buying more and making sure that there was stuff that everyone liked. However, it did mean that there were always ready supplies of the crap that I loved to eat close to hand. The other problem was that Jennie didn't like most of my 'speciality' dishes. When I cooked in the past, I would often do speedy things that didn't take a lot of time. Stir fries were a particular favourite of mine – quick, simple and healthy. Jennie didn't like stir-fried vegetables such as peppers and chillies. Unfortunately, both she and Jodie liked the things I didn't – cauliflower, swede and butternut squash. This often led to a little tension when it came to dinnertime. Moreover, my office was still a good hour's drive away and, by going round the M25, this could easily stretch to two hours if there had been an accident en route. Often when I came home, I really couldn't be bothered to get the pots and pans out and start cooking. So takeaways became an ever more frequent option. It was so easy to slip through the door and pick up the phone.

As we had Jodie to look after, Jennie and I couldn't go out anywhere at night, so I became used to nights in front of the television. Boredom began to creep into my evenings and the best, and only, solution I had found to boredom was to eat. Also, it was becoming very clear that Jennie was my one true soulmate, the person on this earth who I had been destined to find. I was contented, the hideous prospect of spending life on my own had receded into the background, which meant I felt I could relax and be myself. And for me, that meant eating. Because of these factors, I piled weight on. Within six months I had outgrown my clothes and Jennie and I both realised that we had to do something about it. She suggested that we try out Slimming World. To me, this seemed like a ludicrous suggestion, paying money to go to a weekly club with leaders who will simply tell you to eat healthy and do some more exercise. I was also aware that men don't do slimming clubs – the last thing I wanted was to be with a group of women talking about how their 'cycle' affected their weight loss. But I knew that things were once again getting out of control. What Jennie didn't know was that at work I was still up to my old tricks – burgers and chips in the Albert and, with the prospect of a one- to two-hour drive to look forward to, I really stocked up on the crisps and chocolate for the journey home. My major concern about the slimming club was whether they would have scales big enough to accommodate my weight. Jennie made a few phone calls and they said they could weigh people up to 30 stone in weight. I knew I was heavy but I certainly didn't think I was 30 stone, so, after some gentle pushing from Jennie, I agreed to give it a go.

My fears were well founded indeed: I was the only man attending the sessions and it caused a great deal of excitement among the ladies there. 'A man. We've finally got a man!' I heard one say – they must have led very sheltered lives if they were getting excited about me! Having never been to one of these types of meeting before, I didn't really know what to expect. I was sort of imagining a boxing match weigh-in, with all the press cameras flashing as you get on the scales. Of course, it isn't like that at all, you get weighed privately and with dignity, and all the details are recorded in your own little book so you have a record of your progress. I had a bit of a shock, as I was expecting to be around 25 stone. After all, I was a tall man and very solidly built. However, I topped the scales at 27 stone! Yes, the number was a shock, but I wasn't overly concerned, because I was still able to run around with Jodie, visit the gym (albeit it occasionally) and could easily get around nine holes of golf. However, I was determined to get some of the weight off.

The Slimming World diet basically consists of green days and red days, which caused some problems in our household. Green days were Jennie's favourite, these were basically carbohydrate days where you could eat your carbs but couldn't consume protein. Red days were the protein days, where you could eat loads of meat but no carbs – these were my favourite days. So it'll come as no surprise to hear that Jennie always wanted to have green days while I always wanted to stick to the red days. Somehow we managed to come to a compromise and for the first week I stuck to the diet like glue. I think the pressure of having a weigh-in and then a group 'how much did you lose?' session, added to the desire to succeed. So I was hopeful when it came to the weigh-in during our second visit to Slimming World because I suspected that, if I stuck at something, I would lose the weight quickly. I was right: ten pounds came off in that first week. I won my first half a stone sticker – only another 20 more of them to go!

The ladies in the group were very impressed with my achievements, although some were a little annoyed that in one week I'd managed to lose the same amount that it had taken some of them over two months to achieve – but of course they all didn't have the amount of weight to lose that I was facing. We all sat down for our support session, the leader of the group giving us all tips and tricks on how to succeed. Then one lady complained that she had been really good on the diet but still put on weight and I could just sense it coming, I knew just where this conversation was going and I knew it was going to be bad. My fears were realised when the talk turned to 'ladies' issues'. Being the only man in a group of 30 wasn't the most comfortable of scenarios for me in the first place, but, when the discussion was on how the menstrual cycle is likely to affect your weight loss, that hall was the last place on earth I wanted to be. I sank lower in my chair, but the leader ploughed on regardless, oblivious to the fact she actually had a man in the group. Then at the end she suddenly realised I was there and said, 'Of course, none of this is relevant to you, Neil.'

Really? I would never have guessed!

The second week was under way and I was still pretty good at sticking to the diet. The biggest problem I found was at lunchtime, the obvious thing to eat at work (if not going to the pub, of course) was a sandwich. Following the red and green days regime, this meant that you couldn't eat protein and carbohydrate on the same day, which of course made sandwiches completely out of the question. Taking a salad into an office full of blokes going down the pub for two pints and a plate of sausage and mash was a very 'interesting' experience, so on occasions I did transgress. That second week I lost another five pounds which meant I got my first stone sticker! I felt very uncomfortable at the discussion session. I felt all the eyes were on me and I was just waiting for a highly inappropriate discussion to start again.

The next week there wasn't a hope in hell of me sticking to the Sliming World diet. It was time for Flowserve's annual salesforce meeting, this time held in Portugal. The flights were a nightmare – I really had to wedge myself into the seat and then spent five minutes struggling to manage to do up the safety belt. The week just didn't conform to the Slimming World plan, there were no red and green days – just seven beer days. Everyone drank as if it was going out of fashion. It was a good job that there was a ready supply of food – at least I would never have to drink on an empty stomach. But, like the previous year in Dallas, it wasn't all drinking. We did a team-building session which included a long walk around a set course with various tasks such as raft building along the way. We were all given coloured T-shirts to wear in order to define the teams. Despite being a 3XL, mine was skin-tight and, to make things worse, a photographer was on hand to record the event. That evening his photographs were displayed in the lobby of the hotel. There was a hideous shot of me stomping away, big red face, my belly hanging over the top of my trousers and a great big patch of sweat on my back. Strangely, after a few beers in the evening, the photograph mysteriously disappeared from the board –

there were odd reports of a very large man seen running away from the crime scene. There was a round of golf to play one afternoon, and no one had any equipment with them so everything was hired by the company. Unfortunately, Portuguese men clearly aren't very big, as there were no size-13 golfing shoes for me. I squeezed my delicate little footsies into a size 12. This clear discomfort was what I blamed my tee shot on at the first hole, a very nice hook that landed straight in the lake. Why did they have to choose a course with water on it? When playing golf, my ball is always strangely drawn towards the water. This was the first time I had ever used a golf buggy and it's a far easier game when you are not forced to lug your clubs behind you. The only problem with the buggy was that I had trouble driving it, as my stomach kept getting in the way of the steering wheel.

When I returned home, it was pretty clear that, because of the amount of alcohol consumed in Portugal, I had put on weight yet again. So I decided to give it a week before I returned to the Slimming World classes. I couldn't face all of those women knowing that I had put on weight – they would have been so disappointed. But one week became two and then there were quite a few client visits and lunches and then it stretched to three and I just ended up not going back. You might think that I was giving up on this far too easily; after all, I had lost over a stone in just two weeks. It was the group discussion bit that really put me off going back – I think I would have benefited more if there had been men in the group. I tried to stick to the diet without going to the classes, but without the encouragement of the weekly weigh-in there was nothing to keep me on the straight and narrow.

My yo-yoing was actually getting worse. After a period of dieting, like on the Slimming World plan, I would then spend the following weeks being completely and utterly stupid with overindulgent consumption. It was as if I needed to replace the food I felt I had 'missed' during my dieting. Then we heard about this new wonder drug that helped obese people lose weight .It was getting a lot of press, as it had just become available after enjoying some success in the States. Both Jennie and myself made appointments to see our GP.

Amazingly, I had managed to find a GP who was very understanding about obesity, and any health problems were no longer put down just to my being fat. He was also amazed that my blood pressure was practically normal, a strange phenomenon that would thankfully stay with me, even when my weight continued to balloon. My GP had no hesitation in prescribing the pills. Again we encountered the familiar obstacle that he couldn't actually weigh me, but sound reasoning suggested that, if

I couldn't get on the scales, I was probably in need of some help. The pills worked by stopping fat being absorbed into the body. The idea was that about 25 per cent of the fat that you ate would pass straight through you. However, you weren't supposed to eat 'bad' stuff in the first place, otherwise it would make you ill (with diarrhoea, to be blunt). I was very excited by the prospect of these pills; I thought that they might just be the answer to all my problems. Unfortunately, they just added to them.

Things started to go wrong after we had a spaghetti Bolognese for tea. When I wasn't tired from work and the day's adventures on the M25, I actually quite liked cooking. Spaghetti Bolognese was one of my 'speciality' dishes – everything went in the pot: minced beef, chopped tomatoes, onions, mushrooms, garlic, basil and occasionally a pepper or chilli if I could sneak one in without Jennie seeing. Now I would say that this was a pretty healthy dish. I know that mince can be quite fatty but I would always buy the lean version and pour what fat I could away after browning the meat (I sound like a chef here, don't I!). The dish was consumed without incident and then, just before bed, when I was on the computer, I actually crapped myself. No warning, no indication – nothing! Just a quick shot of very orange, very runny shit, all over my clothes and all over the chair. I was mortified! Was I now going to be classed as incontinent? I stuck with the pills for about a month, but every time I went to the loo I would always produce this nasty liquid, an orange mess. If I sneezed or coughed, there was a strong danger of a repeat performance. I lived my life in fear of it happening again and would often walk about with my buttocks clenched – I mean, what would happen if this occurred at work? I wouldn't even say that I ate badly during this period; I simply wouldn't dare for fear of what might happen. It might be argued that this was all going to be worth it, the pill was clearly doing its job and therefore I must be losing weight. But I didn't feel any different and as I couldn't weigh myself I couldn't actually tell if I was losing weight or not. Without that conformation as a motivating factor, it is very difficult to keep on a programme, especially when it is causing such concern. The final straw came one evening when I took off my stone-colour trousers and saw that they were stained bright orange around the bottom region. I had been 'leaking' all day and clearly didn't even notice. It was not an acceptable way to live a life. In order to maintain my dignity, I would have had to wear adult nappies, so I made the decision to stop taking the pills. It took a very long while for the pills to completely come out of my system. Eating my spaghetti Bolognese was always the trigger and, even six months after I'd stopped the course of treatment, I would still suffer the same embarrassing problems on the day I had spag bol for dinner.

The realisation that pills were not going to be my saviour was a very depressing moment. When depression took hold, I turned to my only source of salvation – food. In doing so, I made a bad situation much worse by adding more and more pounds to my body. Then Jennie and me made a decision that was going to take stress, anxiety and pressure to a whole new level – we were going to start a business.

Friday, 20 February 2009

Pre-op assessment day – we've gotta go down to St Richard's again, for a further range of tests before the operation. I'm not sure why they're having to do all this again, surely we did all that when I was in for the sleep assessment. I'm dreading them having to take blood again, I don't fancy an acupuncture session this morning. I've been remarkably calm and relaxed since the phone call two weeks ago informing me that the operation would take place on 4 March. I'm resigned to the fact that what will be will be. All I have to make sure I do is follow their instructions to the letter to give myself the best possible chance.

However, saying all that, last night I was feeling

pretty scared and had another of my moaning sessions to Jennie.

When we arrived, there were loads of people in the waiting area and it was hard to find a seat. There was a man in there who had just recently had the bypass surgery done, and he was telling everyone about it. He was quite a short man and said he had previously been 37 stone. Before they could do the operation he had to have a gastric balloon, which made him lose six stone, and only then were they able to safely complete the procedure. He still looked pretty big but he and his wife were explaining how for the previous ten years their lives had been on hold. I realised that it was much the same for them as it currently is for me and Jennie. He also explained how he had very little pain after the operation, which is a great relief to hear.

There was also a lady called Di in the waiting area who was having the operation the same day as me, so it was nice to know somebody in advance. Jennie and I then had a whirlwind of tests and meetings with various people. Firstly I was weighed again and unfortunately had put back on most of the weight I previously lost. My weight was 272kg. We then met with a staff nurse and filled in the same form I'm sure I did on my last visit. Once again the resuscitation question was asked, and I hoped she ticked the right box. My blood pressure was taken and bizarrely even with white-coat syndrome it was still pretty normal: 154/86. My temperature was also taken and – surprise surprise! – I was a little bit hot, nothing new there, then. We then went to have the blood tests, some walk away from the bariatric area but I managed it OK with only a short rest before we attempted the stairs. The blood area wasn't geared up for bariatrics and I had to perch on the end of the nurse's chair while she got the blood out. Fortunately, she was an experienced phlebotomist and she got the blood first time. Jennie told her that she was brilliant and she said, 'No, dear, I'm not brilliant, just old.' I relaxed a bit more after this as I had really been dreading the blood tests following my experience last time.

We then returned to the bariatric area where yet more people had arrived for clinic. There was another man who didn't really say much but his operation was scheduled for the same day as mine. He also looked very big but, when his turn came to go and get his blood done, he couldn't even walk that far and so had to be taken in a wheelchair. I *know this sounds bad but that made me feel a lot better because if they were going to operate on him then surely I wouldn't have any problems. Another man in the waiting area disappeared into see Mr Salter, the other bariatric surgeon, while his wife told us all that this was his third attempt at having the operation done. The previous occasions he had been too frightened to go through with it. So it looks like I'm not the only one to have these feelings of fear and concern. Next on the itinerary was ten minutes with the dietician. She explained how my stomach would be after the operation: in short, very, very small. I'd only be able to cope with a very small amount of food in one go, and to start with this would need to be mashed up and very soft. We also went through the pre-op milk diet that I'd read about on the Internet. Basically, from now till the operation I wasn't permitted any food at all. I'd have to drink four pints of milk a day and a beef drink (which I can't stand). In addition I could have a small amount of sugar-free jelly and as many sugar-free drinks as I wanted. It looks like I'm going to be peeing for England over the next few days. The purpose of the milk diet is to shrink the liver. In a fat person, the liver is always bigger than normal because it has a lot of fatty tissue in it. So by shrinking the liver the surgeon has a lot more room to do his stuff.*

We then returned to the waiting area to wait for the appointment with the anaesthetist. Another man appeared and he was in a really bad way. He was wearing filthy clothes and his stomach was hanging down to his knees. Poor Jennie had to sit next to him and she told me that he really smelled. This man told the room that he was here on his first session with the consultant, and was waiting for funding. I do hope this man can get the operation done, because he must live a far worse existence than me.

We then had to go and see the anaesthetist. He looked at all my results and I asked if he was concerned about the procedure and he told me that he had no real worries. He said I may be on the heavier side of the people that they operate on, but I was also in reasonably good shape for a 43-stone man and so there shouldn't be any problems. My neck was 53cm and this did represent a small problem in being able to get a tube down my throat. The sleep apnoea might cause another issue, but as these conditions were known about the medical team would be able to manage them.

So it's great news all round really. No one Jennie and I spoke to seems to have any concerns about me having the operation, other than me! And seeing the other people who are going to be operated on and listening to their stories also makes me feel better. I ring Mum to tell her the good news and she is thrilled. Dad, however, is more concerned that he is currently driving through a flood and he thinks he's going to be washed away! Consequently I call him back later. We stop off at the shop on the way home and stock up on milk for the morning. We celebrate with one final takeaway before all of this stops for good.

10
INTO BUSINESS

Jennie had been saying for a while that she wanted to
start her own care agency. She explained that her boss
drove around in a Rolls-Royce and had a beautiful house
while she worked very hard, got the new business in, dealt
with the problems and was on call 24/7! Her salary wasn't
great and she was expected to use her own car to travel to
meetings. Jennie's argument went that, if she was doing it
for her boss, then why not do it for herself? My argument,
however, was what about the salary? What would happen
if no business came in? How would we live on just my
income? Like most decisions in our house, we sat down,
talked about it and decided that Jennie was right all along
– she came straight out of Brian Clough's stable!

A care agency basically supplies care staff to care
homes, hospitals and private people who need assistance.
It does not supply nursing staff because you need a

licence for that. Jennie had been working in this line of business for the previous ten years and had been running one of the biggest care agencies in Essex – she knew the regulations inside out and she knew what clients wanted. It all seemed a sound commercial proposition: there is an ageing population who will always require care and there are also very high numbers of people with learning disabilities who need care – it wasn't a business sector that would be affected by seasonal trends or economic conditions.

We knew that my bonus of six or seven grand would be coming soon and would help to see us through the lean months that would inevitably come as we established our business. We also slowly started collecting various stationery samples from a number of sources, trade shows and the like. Then when Flowserve decided to move office it proved a gold mine for us! The Europe, Middle East and Africa head office was situated just over a mile away in Claygate, so when the lease expired on the office in Esher it made sense for the sales team to move over to join the rest of the company. The building happened to be owned by Cliff Richard, he had the middle floor and we had the top floor. As Cliff was looking to downsize, we switched floors with him. It was actually a very interesting place to work. Cliff had all his gold discs hanging up on the stairs and he was a regular visitor, although of course it meant we left the beloved Albert Arms behind. But the office move proved very useful for us. Jennie and I managed to acquire three different desks, three office chairs and a couple of filing cabinets, together with loads of old lever arch files! It couldn't have happened at a better time. Fortunately, by this stage, I had been 'noted down' as a potential star of the future and had been given a company car. This meant that all my petrol was paid for which was a godsend, as I went back and forth around the M25 transporting furniture.

The plan was that I would continue working at Flowserve, so at least we would be sure of one income coming in each month. Jennie would then quit her job and start work on the business. As Jennie had little knowledge of accounting or standard business practices, I volunteered to look after this aspect, even though I had about as much clue as a headless chicken. I read up on payroll, software, factoring, VAT, bank charges, profit and turnover – it was a very good way to fall asleep at night. For about three months we plotted and planned, I registered a limited company, researched payroll and accounting software, arranged banking requirements and began to look around for offices. Jennie did all of her side of things – mainly writing forms, policies and a million and one other requirements and safeguards that are needed if you are thinking about starting a care-based business. We also did a bit of research about competitors; we got a fax installed on our phone line and rang up other agencies saying that we were about to set up a care home and would need agency cover, so could they send us their prices – two minutes later we would have a fax giving us all of our competitors' pricing. A cunning trick I've used extensively over the years! Then Jennie would go and have an 'interview' with these same care staff on the understanding that she was looking for care work. This way we found out what they paid their staff. Conducting research in this way was key to our success, because by knowing the staff pay rates we could then offer a more attractive package to encourage their staff to join our agency instead. When Jennie went for her 'interviews', she found some appalling practices going on. In one interview, Jennie was offered a shift that very afternoon – no police check, no references, nothing! She could have been a murderer just out of prison for killing old people on a previous care job! We vowed that we would be different.

Finally, we were in position to launch our master plan and Jennie handed in her notice. She had to work four weeks' notice and her firm literally begged her to stay, so we negotiated another two weeks at a decent rate in order to boost our bank balance for a while. We also found a small office above a shop at the top of Tonbridge high street. The rent was £350 a month which doesn't seem a lot compared to the rents we pay now, but we really weren't getting much for our money. However, if things didn't work out at least there was no notice period. After much hassle I had managed to get telephones installed – an unbelievably complicated task! I had found a company that you could rent a copier from without a long-term contract (there must surely be a business opportunity for someone there!). Moving into the office was fun – access was up a rickety old fire escape at the back and then we had to go up in to the attic space. I almost killed myself there and then when my size-13s slipped on the narrow stairs and a filling cabinet ended up landing on top of me.

Finally, the time came when Jennie was due to start the business on a full-time basis – so now, no salary was coming in. She spent a week or so in the new office and decided she didn't like it. I hung my head in despair! The problem was she had no one to bounce ideas off – a problem when you are trying to get new business in. So she took on her old assistant manager from the previous company on a three-day-a-week basis. Looking back, it was a completely and utterly mad decision. How could we even think to employ someone when we didn't have any business coming in? Not only were we not getting business, we also had very few care staff on the books in case a shift did come in. So we made a decision that we wouldn't just target business in Kent, we would widen our net and target business in Essex too, business of course that Jennie knew well. So we hosted a recruitment day in Southend and held the interviews in the garden of our new employee, Jane. We simply placed a very small advert in the local paper, nothing more, and amazingly 80 people turned up. So different from Kent where we had only managed to get four people on the books in three weeks. Then the work flooded in – and suddenly I started to have work to do.

I needed to invoice the client for the work done, send the invoice over to the factoring company who would then advance us 70 per cent of the invoice value, then the following week I would have to run the payroll and telephone the bank to actually make the payment. This was fine for the first few weeks, as there were only one or two invoices to handle. But rapidly it built up to a mammoth task. Thursdays were invoicing days, so I would get back to Tonbridge from Esher at around six (as long as the M25 played ball, that was), and then go straight to our small office where I would do the invoicing for two or three hours. Then the following Tuesday I would have to run the payroll system and telephone through all the details to the bank to make the payments – I'd get home at about 10pm. These were high-pressure tasks, as if we didn't invoice and get the correct paperwork back to the factoring company in time there was no way that we would have the money available to pay our staff's wages the following week. If I got a member of staff's wages wrong, then all hell would break loose. These were all tasks that I was learning step by step. I had never been near an accounts department in the past before – when I joined Envirotech I had to ask what an invoice was, I was so naive! I also had to ensure that VAT returns were completed, Inland Revue payments made on time, not to mention all the bills! In those early days, we made some great choices, the office was pretty cheap, the photocopier was not tied down to a long-term contract and all the furniture was either second-hand or free. However, we also made some pretty bad ones, the telephone and mobile phone deals were abysmal, the banking charges were not negotiated at all and you would not believe the price that we paid for business cards!

It was a steep learning curve and we lived and breathed the business. Even when Jennie was at home in the evenings and weekends, the business would come with her via the 'on call' system on the mobile. As a care agency we were on call 24 hours a day, 7 days a week. The phone calls would start at about 5.30am, as care homes realised that they were short of staff for the early shift, and the phone rarely stopped ringing until 10.30pm when all the night shifts were finally sorted out. The major problem was covering the shifts; you'd get a requirement for a shift that started within 45 minutes of the call and then have to start ringing around the staff on the books to try to get it covered. In spite of the stress, it was great fun and the thrill of the phone ringing with more work was fantastic. After a few months, in addition to Jane, we recruited a second part-time booking consultant, as well as a part-time salesman. With the salesman on board, we were getting new homes contacting us virtually on a daily basis, which was great. We were holding recruitment day after recruitment day – all at the weekend and all at Jane's house. After about the fourth of these recruitment days, there was a knock on Jane's door – it was the police. They wanted to find out what was going on. So many people had been coming to the property over the last month, they thought she was running a drug den! The amount of work that was coming in was very exciting. After our fifth recruitment day in two months we were driving home from Southend and no less than four new care homes rang up offering us shifts – Jennie couldn't even get a break in the car.

As exciting as this all was, it was extremely time-consuming and very stressful. Poor Jodie mustn't have got a lot of attention those first few months and by the age of seven she could probably have covered shifts at nursing homes and rung up the bank to make wage payments.

As I was flying around the country, Esher – Tonbridge – Southend, basically working two jobs seven days a week, there wasn't a lot of time for cooking. We would still have a varied diet though: Indian one night, then a Chinese, then pizza, then kebabs and finally fish and chips. True to form, my coping mechanism kicked in whenever the stress levels rose, and I'd eat even more than usual. Fortunately, Internet shopping had arrived at Tesco. So now I could get my fix delivered straight to my door, without having to go to the trouble of walking round the shop, fantastic news for the time-poor Bakewell household. I was becoming even more sedentary than before, I passed on golf at work because of having to run the payroll and when at home in the evenings I was simply sitting down to do even more work. I was being fuelled by pure adrenaline at times – well, adrenaline and Coke. I was drinking even more of the fizzy black stuff than ever, after about 10am I would always have a can of it on my desk. I would guess that I was going through something like 10 or 12 cans of it a day. Then at night I would have trouble sleeping because of acid reflux caused by the sheer level of acid that my system must have produced trying to process such an unhealthy quantity of cola. My suits for work had become really tight, so I just wore those for meetings with important clients, while in the office I wore more comfortable trousers and a shirt. However, the trousers were pretty casual in nature so, after a week or so, I was called up about it by my boss. I had no choice but to locate a new suit that would actually fit me. For years I had been shopping at 'fat shops', as I called them, or to give them their proper name, outsized gentlemen's outfitters. Jennie and I located one in nearby Tunbridge Wells and went in to purchase a new suit. I was stunned to see that my waist measurement was now up to 58 inches. No wonder that my old stuff wasn't fitting properly. We came out with a nice new suit, but £400 down! Yet another problem of being fat is that clothing is so bloody expensive!

On the plus side, the money from the care business was coming in thick and fast, and we were taking around £15K a week. It sounds a lot but most of it would go straight back out again in staff wages and National Insurance. It was becoming harder and harder for me to cope, rushing home to do the invoicing and the payroll – these were things that had to be done on a weekly basis so it was a constant cycle of administration work. We bought another computer and a desk and installed them in our bedroom at home. At least this way I didn't have to spend my whole evenings alone in the small office without seeing either Jennie or Jodie. But what the business really needed was someone to take control of the finances on a full-time basis. We began to discuss the possibility of my handing in my notice at work to commit to our business full-time.

Sunday, 22 February 2009

Second day of the milk diet. It's not as tough as I thought it was going to be. Trying to drink four pints of milk a day is surprisingly difficult, I don't think I have managed the full amount yet. The only thing I am doing is thinking about food a lot. I dream up various cooked breakfast combinations, I love a good cooked breakfast.

The only problem is, I didn't get on very well with the beef drink. I've never liked gravy or any sort of sauce on food and now I'm being asked to basically drink something like gravy direct from the cup. Quite frankly it tastes like shit! Hopefully by the time I have the operation I'll have lost well over a stone or perhaps even more. Surely I've got to drop weight pretty quickly if I'm not eating anything. As expected I'm making regular trips to the loo. I've never peed so much in my life. Surprisingly I'm still having to visit the toilet to poo as well, I thought this would all stop but maybe I've still got a lot of food left in my system.

Jennie has taken on the cooking role (much to her disgust). Last night when Dad and Siobhan were here, she cooked sausages and mash. She was very proud of herself and told me she didn't burn the sausages like me and also she managed to cook without making a mess. I was thrilled for her. The hardest part of all this is the smell of the food being cooked and eaten around me. I can never get away from these delicious cooking smells and wonder if it might have been easier for me to move out while on this diet. Jennie has been very good and is not eating around me. Jodie, on the other hand, seems to delight in showing me her plate of food at every available opportunity. I guess the next week or so will only get harder after all there is only so long that you can go without food. The one thing I've got to do is rigidly stick to this diet for the remaining eight days. I can't afford to slip off because then that will endanger my chances in the operation.

Jennie's *decree absolut* finally came through and I was no longer living with a married woman! We had talked about getting married for some time as getting engaged was one of Jennie's favourite topics of conversation. I had told her there was no way that I was going to propose while she was still married – so now that the divorce papers had come through I had no more excuses left. I made arrangements for the 'on-call' to be handled by one of our employees for the weekend. Jodie was going to her father's so I took the Friday afternoon off work and went up to our office to surprise Jennie. I took a big bunch of white roses with me and whisked her off to a nice hotel in the countryside for a couple of nights. There on that first afternoon during a walk in the gardens I proposed. I did it in the proper manner – down on one knee and everything. Fortunately, she said yes.

One of the most bizarre experiences of my life happened that evening. We were sat in the restaurant having a romantic meal for two, celebrating our engagement like any normal couple. The whole of the restaurant was empty and then through the door walked 20 very large Japanese men dressed in suits, accompanied by a similar number of very petite Japanese ladies kitted out in traditional dress. Had we walked into some kind of Jeremy Beadle-type *Game for a Laugh* situation? Then two English guys appeared, both in blazers with the words 'Sumo Association' emblazoned on the breast pocket. Not many people can say that on the night of their engagement they dined with 20 sumo wrestlers. Jennie was panicking that they were going to come over and ask me to join their team.

The following day we went to buy the ring. I was extremely patient as I was dragged from one shop to the next and then, inevitably, we returned and bought the first ring we had seen in the first shop we visited. This was also the first time I remember Jennie getting pissed off because people were staring at me. We had nipped into a newsagent close to the hotel to pick up something. While I was paying, Jennie was flicking through magazines. An old women and her daughter came in and apparently the old women had looked me up and down and whispered, 'Ooh...look at the size of him!'

Jennie responded with a few well-chosen words of wisdom for the lady: 'What's wrong with you? Have you never seen a big person before?'

This left the old woman gob-smacked and me highly embarrassed. A similar thing happened at breakfast the following morning. It was one of those buffet breakfasts that you so often get in hotels these days, I'd just finished a starter of fresh fruit and got up to tackle the main business of the full English. When I returned to the table, Jennie was staring intently at a couple on the other side of the restaurant and as I sat down she gave them a very sarcastic smile and a 'Can I help you?' Apparently, they had stared at me from the moment I got up, watched me put every item of food on my plate and then followed me till I sat down, to be met by the icy stare of Jennie when they looked away. Jennie was always very bothered by the stares that I got and always rushed in, as she was more comfortable being confrontational than I have ever been. I had never noticed people staring at me before, apart from the occasional child who looked up at me in awe. I must have been oblivious to the amount of weight I had now put on. For me at the breakfast table that morning, Jennie's confrontational stance made the whole matter worse and made me even more embarrassed. Stares were going to become a regular part of my life, it was something that I – and more importantly Jennie – was going to have to get used to.

The wedding was planned for the following June so we got our heads down, cracking on with the business of getting it organised. I began to fill a little bit unwell, I occasionally got chest pains – nothing major, just the little twinge now and then. The workload at Flowserve was immense at that time, as the company had just taken over another major firm and was integrating numerous factory sites. This meant that customers' spare parts were being delayed and being delayed big time, so every single day I was going in to work and being shouted out by customers who were less than impressed with the company's efforts. Couple this with the amount of work going on back home – I was probably stressed up to high heaven. After mentioning this to a few office friends, they said I should go and see the doctor who would probably sign me off and I would get a few weeks' rest and relaxation. Not being one to do 'sick' at the best of times, this wasn't me at all and I pooh-poohed the idea. However, when over in Holland for a few days to help with the integration process of a factory out there, I experienced a very worrying development. After a busy day of meetings, I had a nap on the bed before going down for dinner. Waking up and realising that time was cracking on, I leaped up. The thing was, my legs weren't on the same wave length as my brain and I just ended up collapsing in a crumpled heap on the floor. It was petrifying – I didn't have a clue what was wrong. After 15 minutes of lying on the floor, I finally summoned the courage and dragged myself up on to the bed and gradually stood up. I was very shaky on my feet for the next couple of days – more likely to do with the fear of something untoward happening rather than any physical problem.

This incident led me to rethink my aversion to visiting my GP and off I went. He asked me questions about my workload and asked if I ever felt down because of my weight. I realised that, actually, yes, I did feel down about my size, my health and my general lifestyle. When he asked me if I ever felt suicidal, I realised that he too thought I was stressed and depressed. I did almost laugh at the question, as suicide was never something that had crossed my mind (well, apart from when England lost a Test Match). The doctor concluded that I was working too hard and signed me off sick for just over two weeks.

I felt terribly guilty. Having been someone who had only taken about two days off sick in four years of work, this state of affairs was something that was completely alien to me. There was also no way that I could stop doing my tasks for our business – the whole enterprise would just collapse – so it was Flowserve that really suffered with my two weeks of absence. I did try to take it a little easy during the times that I wasn't required to run any payroll or do invoices. I lay on the sofa one afternoon, unheard of for me, and 'bang' the sofa collapsed underneath me. I rushed upstairs to find some books to prop it up with, not admitting what happened to Jennie until many weeks later. God knows how much weight I had put on if I was now breaking sofas. I remember the date of that incident quite clearly – it was 11 September 2001. Together with the rest of the world, I watched with horror the attacks in America. They put my problems into context. What those two weeks off did was show me that being able to complete my role in the business during the day as opposed to the evenings was far more productive, far less stressful and actually better for the business. I could answer questions from staff members about their pay and communicate better with the factoring company about unpaid invoices and client queries. This realisation, combined with the stress and hassle of working at Flowserve increasing, meant that, as soon as Jennie and I could afford it, I wanted to hand in my notice and come and work for the business full-time.

Over the winter, I got a cough. Not unusual in winter of course, but I couldn't shift this one for love or money. I'd had something similar in university where I seemed to have a silly little cough for about four months. But this cough was something else, plus it was really getting me down. It was heavy and hacking and that seemed to drain my energy like nothing else. I couldn't sleep properly at night and would often go into heavy coughing fits. There was also the added complication that during a heavy coughing fit I was fearful of crapping myself again. Ever since trying the medication to lose weight, I felt that things weren't completely right 'around the back'. It was as if the normal muscles wouldn't work properly. On occasion, if I had a heavy cough or a sudden sneeze, things would 'let go' and I would slightly soil myself. It was terribly embarrassing, not something a young man in his twenties should be worrying about. Then the coughing fits began to have an even worse effect. I suddenly started to feel funny after some of my fits, as if I was in a different place and would then suddenly appear back in reality feeling all spaced out. It was strange and I couldn't put my finger on what was happening. Finally after one really bad bout, it suddenly came to me: I was actually passing out from lack of oxygen. I didn't consider it a problem as I put it down to stress, but in reality it was actually quite dangerous, what would happen if I had a coughing fit and passed out while driving or while I was standing up and fell over and cracked my head? But, instead of seeking help, I ploughed on regardless.

Weddings were in the air. Jennie was racing away with the plans for our nuptials, but my best friend Matthew was going to beat me to it. He had met his bride-to-be during his time at Leeds University and, as the couple were still living in Leeds, the wedding was held up there. I was asked to be best man, which of course I readily accepted. But this, of course, meant that I would need the appropriate clothing. Morning suits were ordered for the occasion and, as we couldn't lay our hands on a tape measure, I simply told the shop assistant get the biggest items he could find. I wisely packed a pair of my own trousers, knowing damn well that the pair supplied wouldn't be big enough. It was a prudent move. I managed to squeeze into the jacket, but the waistcoat didn't have a chance in hell of fitting. So there I was doing best man duties, in an assortment of clothing and lacking certain key items – yet another humiliating experience for the fat man!

The time I spent off work really got me thinking. Did I really want to be driving for at least an hour every day just to get to work? Did I really want the grief that my customers gave me? Did I want to be reporting to a boss every day for the rest of my life? Wouldn't it just be better to quit and work to develop the business in partnership with Jennie? The answer was of course yes.

Then a curve ball was thrown into the equation. Corporate headquarters in Dallas was looking for a number of promising people across the world to undergo a black belt six sigma programme. Six sigma is a business management strategy that is utilised by many of the world's leading corporations. It helps improve business practice and streamline processes. The black belt was its top standard. The European salesforce was asked to select someone for this programme, and that someone was me! The training would take place at various locations throughout the world and afterwards it would certainly have led to a senior management position, again, throughout the world. I had to think long and hard about what I wanted out of life. This was a fantastic opportunity, a chance to climb the corporate ladder, see the world and make myself highly employable for the rest of my life. But it was impossible! Jennie may well have followed me to the four corners of the globe, but I couldn't justify to myself the upheaval it would cause Jodie. It wouldn't be fair to ship her from country to country as I was appointed on different projects – I couldn't expect her to start a new school every couple of years. And what would happen to our fledgling business? It was Jennie's new baby – I couldn't ask her to pull herself away from that. So, in an act of selflessness, I declined their kind invitation, and a month or so later handed in my resignation.

Now I was on board full-time, we needed a new office. Our first little one had served us well but now we needed bigger premises in order to expand the way we wanted. We decided that because the majority of our Kent-based business was in the Medway area we would get a unit over there. The advantage of this was that we would be closer to care staff, plus rental prices were a damn sight cheaper than in Tonbridge. We found an ideal office suite with an office for Jennie, one for me, a large open plan area and a room in which to train our staff. Moving offices was a nightmare. I really struggled with all the lifting and physical work. I couldn't remember the last time I had done any exercise and it was beginning to show – my breathing was so laboured. With the help of our staff, we finally managed it and, with a set of new executive furniture in my new, river-view office, I really thought that I had arrived.

15 June 2002 was finally here. It was a very important date. England were playing Denmark in the World Cup finals – oh, yes, and I was getting married! Jennie and I had decided on a civil service in a local country house. We didn't hold back – we had the works: marquees, string quartets, fine wines, I had even had a waistcoat made for the occasion! Jennie looked stunning in her wedding

gown and Jodie had the courage to read out a beautiful poem. It had taken some planning, a lot of heartache and a not inconsiderable amount of stress, as I had to give the dressmaker a few well-chosen words a week beforehand as the dress was nowhere near ready. Our wedding breakfast was followed by the dreaded speeches – hardly my strong point because of my stutter. In spite of this drawback, my speech went well and I only really stuttered once throughout the whole thing. As well as the wedding breakfast, we had a massive buffet in the evening but everyone seemed more interested in dancing and drinking by then and there was a ton of food left over. It was a lovely day, but I think it's fair to say we were both glad when we could finally escape at the end of it. We were both so knackered, there was absolutely no chance of the normal wedding-night activities – I think that we were both asleep as our heads touched the pillows.

It was fair to say that we were both completely washed out. The last 12 months had been an absolute whirlwind both emotionally and physically. As we stood on the deck of the ship on our honeymoon cruise, we were both so glad to finally get a break from the stresses and pressures of normal everyday life.

Unfortunately, the stresses and pressures were soon going to come back, and for a long time. With them, my weight was going explode at a rate that even I had never seen before.

11
LIMITED LIFE

O ur honeymoon was ten days of pure bliss. It was great to finally get away from ringing phones, the pressure of a payroll and constantly living and breathing the business. It's fair to say that the stress of the wedding arrangements had also got to us and we were both relieved it was finally all over. The cruise was amazing, it was like staying in a five-star hotel where the view changed every single day. Jennie and I could sit back, enjoy the sun and most importantly enjoy food around the clock! Cruising is not a holiday you want to go on if you are thinking about trying to keep the pounds off – you can literally eat from dawn to dusk if you so wish. We enjoyed the cruise so much, the first thing we did when we got home was to book another one for later in the year.

The business was beginning to grow at an

unbelievable rate. With the move over to Medway, we finally began to break heavily into the Kent marketplace. This new level of business meant more office-based staff and the monthly payroll seemed to be increasing every month. The stress of having to meet this payroll every month lay heavily on my shoulders. Trying to make sure that our clients paid us on time was almost impossible! Because of this we started delaying payments to our own suppliers in order to have sufficient funds to meet the payroll. Of course, when in paid employment, I never even thought about these things – I just simply took it for granted that the money would be there. When you have to find it yourself, it's a completely different matter. Of course, stress is my worst trigger for eating. I handle it badly and the first thing I turn to is food.

Unfortunately, as soon as we moved into the new office, we found that there was a sandwich van doing the rounds. Yes, he was convenient, but he did no good for my waistline. I ended up often spending £10 a day on the van man. He would normally arrive at about 10am, so hot sausage rolls were bought as a mid-morning snack, then a sandwich or roll with crisps, chocolate and Coke for lunchtime! With this mid-morning arrival, I developed a new habit. I'd eat my sausage roll, and then ten minutes later find myself tucking into the sandwich I'd bought for lunch. Within an hour the entire pile of food I had purchased had disappeared. So at lunchtime, I decided that I was hungry again and dispatched someone to go and buy me a sandwich from the local shop. It seemed as though, whenever food was in my sight, I was compelled to eat it there and then – as though someone was going to take it away from me. I had absolutely no willpower to resist it.

This problem began to snowball and would soon apply to all aspects of my eating. When most people order a takeaway and they feel full, they simply stop eating. Not me. I'd ensure that every single last bit was eaten and then I'd also make sure everyone else had eaten their portions – if not I'd soon polish those off as well. Soon enough, I couldn't eat just one biscuit, I'd have to go through the whole packet until nothing was left in front of me. The weekly shopping would arrive and half of it would be gone within 24 hours. It was crazy. But I simply couldn't stop myself from doing it. If ever I was in doubt that I had a form of addiction, this behaviour surely confirmed it. I did have my doubts about this so-called addiction theory. I suppose in many ways I still do to a certain degree. At times I thought myself to be a greedy, lazy, useless slob, and that this was the only reason why I had got myself to this size. My personal self-loathing was never far away. The only thing I could do to make that anger and hatred at myself go away was to indulge still further.

After we returned from honeymoon, we decided that, as time was ticking, certainly with Jennie's biological clock, we really wanted to try for a baby. To be honest, for quite a while Jennie had been 'forgetting' to take her pill, but nothing had happened to date. So we decided to put a great deal of effort into the process! The first night of this task Jennie found out about the sofa I had broken the previous year when it collapsed in a heap underneath us! I was forced into a full and frank confession. We tried all the tricks in the book, with Jennie even trying the old trick of putting her legs up the wall for half an hour or so afterwards, but nothing happened. I was beginning to get worn out. My fitness wasn't what it used to be. So after a great debate one night which saw Jennie in floods of tears, we decided to book an appointment to see our GP. Talking to the doctor about my sex life isn't what I would consider to be a jolly way to pass a morning, but it was something I couldn't really avoid.

We actually knew that our chances of success were going to be limited because Jennie had had part of one of her tubes removed following an ectopic pregnancy in her previous marriage. After a short and highly embarrassing discussion, the doctor sent me for all the appropriate tests. As for many men who have been in this position, producing the required sample was not easy. In fact, it was incredibly stressful. How on earth I managed it I still don't know. Then we had to get the sample to the hospital while keeping it warm. So Jennie kept the sample bottle in her bra as we raced in the car to the hospital. Handing in the sample was also a very humiliating experience, especially when the person logging it all in told me that there wasn't very much there, but that they'd do the best they could.

My fears were realised when the results came back. The sperm I had were fine – both of them! But my sperm count was extremely low, so low that the doctor said it was likely that Jennie would get pregnant when there was a blue moon and a squadron of pigs doing a night-time flyby mission. We were told that my obesity was a significant factor in my less-than-impressive count. Being fat increases the oestrogen count, which lowers the level of testosterone, and coupled with the fact that fat people tend to be hotter means that there is very little chance of sperm being produced. It was something that I was expecting. I think I had known in my heart of hearts that something wasn't right for quite a long time. Even though I knew what the test results were going to show, it still hit me like a brick in the face. It's stupid – but you feel less of a man because of it.

Not being able to fulfil the basic requirements of a husband had a negative impact on my mental health. This on top of the stress caused by the business meant that I started to fall asleep a lot of the time at home. I'd be in my chair at night and I'd just doze off. I also started lying in bed a lot longer than normal in the mornings. All my life I'd been used to getting up with the dawn but now, at weekends, I'd be in bed till 10 or 11 o'clock in the morning. Maybe it was a touch of depression or maybe it was just the start of my sleep apnoea, but, whatever it was, it wasn't pleasant. Whenever I was awake, I would eat a little more, just to make the bad thoughts go away for a while.

At least something good was about to happen: we were going on another cruise! But there was a problem that needed to be solved before we could go. Cruises require male guests to wear suits and formal dinner wear. I didn't have a proper dinner suit and, on our honeymoon, I'd had to wear a normal lounge suit with a bow tie so I'd felt a little out of place. I arranged for a tailor to visit the house to measure me up for some new kit. I did warn him that I was a little on the large side but when he arrived he almost had a heart attack. After measuring me and doing his sums he gave me the price. It was my turn to almost have a heart attack. It took him a while to make, I think his seamstress had difficulty getting the things through the sewing machine. But at least I was now fully kitted up. The cruise was hugely enjoyable and it was great to take Jodie this time, but there were still a number of problematic incidents. Firstly, in the restaurant, all the seating had arms. For most people this wouldn't be an issue but for me it was a nightmare to attempt to squeeze in. In fact, I simply couldn't manage it so on the first night we had to go through the performance of the waiting staff parading a chair with no arms through the 500-seater restaurant as I stood at the table with everyone watching me. Delightful! However, the most embarrassing incident was still to come. Prior to the cruise, I had also visited the 'fat shop' to buy a few items of casual clothing. Jennie selected a very light shirt that would be ideal for a hot, fat man on a cruise. The only thing was, it was an extremely loud shirt – I personally hated it, but, as I was now checking in at a 6XL top, I wasn't what you might call spoiled for choice. I was wearing this shirt on a casual evening aboard ship, when after dinner we decided to go and take in the show. We sat on the very front row because of my long legs. However, these were theatre-style seats and about 30 seconds before the performance started my seat gave way beneath me and I ended up sitting on the floor. So not only had I been made to stand in front of 500 people as a special chair was carried in, but I'd also broken a chair in front of 500 people, this time wearing a very loud shirt!

We hadn't given up on the baby idea. When we got back home, we were sent to see an IVF specialist which entailed yet more uncomfortable sex-related discussion with strangers – great! Unfortunately, my size proved to be a problem again. As my Body Mass Index was over their cut-off level, they wouldn't be able to fund the treatment. Again, another heavy body blow to my confidence and self-esteem. But not only did I feel useless and ashamed, I also felt anger, a lot of anger! I felt the decision was basically saying that if you are fat then you can't be a parent. You aren't suitable for bringing up a child, what could you possibly offer a young human life? Maybe, deep inside, I felt that myself.

So we changed tack and looked into adoption, but it was only a very brief look. I'm surprised that anyone ever fulfils the criteria! Our lifestyle was completely the opposite of what the local authorities required. Both husband and wife working, both with heavy workloads, Jennie smoked and of course I was fat. Being fat is a complete and utter no-go when it comes to adoption, so that put us completely out of the running.

It took me quite a while to get over this knockback. Emotionally, it was a very demanding time. I couldn't help but feel that I had failed my wife for the simple reason of being fat. This, together with the ever-increasing demands of the business, meant that my mind was in turmoil. I began sleeping fitfully, the thoughts of recent events twirling around in my head. This meant that my 'snoozes' in the chair became longer and more frequent. It was at this time that I should have done something drastic about losing weight once and for all.

I should have had the surgery; in fact, a medical professional told me it was the only way that I would lose weight.

Jennie and I hoped that, if I lost a bit of weight, my sperm count might go up and that blue moon might just rise one night, or in a worst case we might creep into the criteria for IVF. So we again approached the doctor (he must have been fed up with the sight of us) who referred us to a dietician. Now I thought that I was getting somewhere. After a bit of a wait, we met a trained professional who no doubt encountered eating disorders – let's face it, I had an eating disorder – on a daily basis. I thought that they would be able to understand my problem and offer help and counselling along the way. I really hoped that this might be a solution or at the very least the light at the end of a long and frightening tunnel. Regretfully not. In fact, she was about as much use as a chocolate fire guard; no, in fact, less use – at least I would have been able to eat the chocolate fire guard to mask the misery of meeting her. Firstly, she spoke very slowly as if I had the intelligence of a five-year-old: clearly, she firmly had it in her mind that fat meant stupid. She also equated our eating habits to that of the Royle Family. When Jennie and I came home from a hard slog in the office, we would eat in front of the telly, it's true, but she was the most patronising woman I had ever had the misfortune to meet, with no understanding of the issues involved, or evident concern or compassion for my situation. Her only gem of helpful advice was that we should eat dinner at a table. Not quite the weight-loss method of the century! In fact, the 'meeting' was less than ten minutes long and basically, after realising that we mainly ate our meals in front of the television, the dietician decided that my only chance of losing weight was by having surgery. We left the meeting shell-shocked. I was angry and felt like complaining about her attitude; Jennie was reduced to tears over the way we had been treated. We had thought that this was going to be such a positive encounter, but it was a total letdown. I was fuming, how dare this ignorant woman suggest that the only way I could lose weight was by having surgery? I was determined to prove her wrong.

Unfortunately, ultimately she was right.

Instead of going down the weight-loss surgery route, I decided to employ the services of a personal trainer. I convinced myself that my weight problems were purely down to my sedentary lifestyle. I refused to accept that the amount of food I was shoving down my throat and the quantities of sugar-laden fizzy pop I was sloshing down afterwards were the factors to address. I had become so used to eating such gargantuan volumes of food that what passed for normal was no longer shocking or disgusting. I simply couldn't see that I was eating so much more than normal people. So, by naively addressing the issue of exercise, I expected the weight to fall off me.

The sessions were booked three days a week after work. It was going to cost a fortune but if it got my weight down, it was going to be worth it. Especially if it meant Jennie and I would then qualify for the IVF treatment, so we both signed up. A key factor was to try to get me walking more, as the increased weight I was carrying was severely limiting the distances I could comfortably walk. I had noticed myself beginning to develop habits that would reduce the amount of walking I would have to do. The principal one was circling a car park until a space became free right next to where I needed to go, anything so I wouldn't have to drag my body about for so long.

Training sessions would start with a small warm up, then we would either go for a short walk or do an aerobics workout. I was never keen on the aerobics, but it was what Jennie enjoyed and keeping her motivated with the exercise was a key part to my own personal success. We would then end our sessions with a short weights session and some abdominal exercises. Certainly my fitness improved with the training – it couldn't really fail to – but my weight showed no signs of changing. As soon as the trainer was out of the door, I would be on the phone ordering a takeaway, feeling far too knackered to cook. I still refused to accept that what I was eating was at the root of the problem, it was something that would take me a long time to get to grips with.

As beneficial as these sessions were for my fitness, if not my weight, I started to get slack. I would end up working late and have to cancel my allotted slot with the trainer far more often than not. I ended up paying for more sessions that we didn't do than those we did. I persevered for about a year, sometimes doing one session a week, sometimes all three. But it made not one bit of difference to my weight. So I finally decided to knock the sessions on the head – it seemed that I was paying out with no real gain. Of course, I was completely to blame – not the trainer. A period of intense exercise two or three times a week wasn't going to be enough to burn off the calories I was consuming on a daily basis, let alone burn off any excess weight. In fact, during the time we had the trainer, I probably put on weight. So I opted for another approach.

By this stage I had completely given up on the baby idea, it was obvious to me that I wouldn't be able to get my weight sufficiently under control to be able to qualify for treatment. So many people get hung up about having babies and fall into deep depression, which was something I wanted to avoid. So I put my thoughts about the subject to the back of my mind and tried to detach myself from it all as much as possible – I consoled myself with the fact that at least I was a good stepfather to Jodie. And I had something to keep my mind occupied: we were going to get our own house.

Me and Jennie found a wonderful three-storey townhouse in a beautiful rural area and fortunately the bank agreed to give us the mortgage. Having rented for so many years, it was a great feeling to finally own bricks and mortar. Inevitably, on moving-in day, I realised just how much my health had declined. I just didn't have the energy to help with any of the tasks we faced. Packing up boxes and doing a clear-out on our rented house almost killed me. I had to keep stopping all the time because I was really feeling pain in my lower back whenever I stood up. Clearly, this was because of the massive amount of weight I was carrying around my front. When we moved into the new house, we wanted to paint everything to our tastes, as opposed to living with the plain magnolia walls that greeted us. But, again, I just couldn't do anything that required standing up for any great length of time. So I was reduced to 'sitting-down' jobs – it was very frustrating for both me and Jennie and I felt that I wasn't fulfilling my role as the man of the house.

I then had a car crash. Nothing that major – I was able to drive home afterwards, but it did more damage than I first realised. I was driving on the motorway when a car hit me from behind. I don't know how it happened, but I got a hell of a shunt. Immediately afterwards I felt no ill effects at all and my major concern was getting the insurance claim sorted out. Then the next morning, my body ached and my feet and hands were all tingling. I paid a visit to the doctor who told me there was little they could do, there was no obvious injury and the discomfort in my fingers would pass within a short period of time. He was right, it did, but my back got a whole lot worse. That summer, I could barely do anything physical. Whenever we went out as a family, I would have to find somewhere for me to sit down to get the pressure off my back. This meant that our trips out became very limited. In fact, my whole life became extremely limited. With the lack of movement, I managed to pile on even more weight. Food soon became my only source of pleasure as I became a prisoner in my own body.

Wednesday, 26 February 2009

One week to go! Hopefully by this time next week everything will be done and I'll be taking the first steps to recovery. Or failing that it will all be over and everyone else can get on with the rest of their lives. I am settling into a routine with the milk diet but I'm sure that by the end of next week I'm never going to want to see another glass of milk again. I've given up with the beef drinks. I just can't stand them. You're meant to have them in order to get a little bit of salt into your system, but I'm sorry, I'm just going to have to do without. I can't possibly face another one.

The guys at work have been very good about not eating around me but now it doesn't seem to bother me so much. Jennie has done very well with the cooking. I thought she'd be on takeaways every night but she hasn't, so maybe we can enter her for MasterChef next year! And she can do her signature dish of chicken and cous cous.

I'm surprised. I thought the milk regime would leave me with very little energy but if anything it's the opposite and I have more than usual. I can feel that my clothes have got a bit looser and I'm walking up the stairs a little bit easier. Maybe it's only psychological but I definitely feel that I've lost weight.

As time ticks closer to the operation, I order a set of pyjamas from the fat-man clothes shop. Pyjamas are something I would never normally wear but as I'm going into hospital I thought I'd better make the effort. I feel like a 70-year-old man in them but I guess I won't be wearing them for long. I also get my *other stuff together for the stay. I'm not really going to need a lot as with any luck I won't be in for too long and will want to get home as soon as possible. I am not doing a lot at work; my mind really isn't on it. I will be glad when all this is done and I can get back to doing a good hard day's work. My thoughts about food seemed to have eased a bit: I have downgraded from fantasies about cooked breakfast to mere cheese and biscuits.*

12
WASTE OF SPACE

The idea of killing myself went through my mind many times over the following years. But to all intents and purposes such dark thoughts were a waste of time. I was already dead.

It's amazing how quickly I accepted my condition. I seemed to forget the things that I used to be able to do, simple things like going for a walk or enjoying time with friends. I soon settled into a deep, dark, cavernous rut. Trying to climb out wasn't an option. I was warm and comfortable and my rut was filled with lots of exciting food-related goodies. I was going nowhere for a while.

My 6XL shirts soon became a 7XL and soon the smart tailored clothes I'd recently had made were consigned to the back of the wardrobe. Tracksuit bottoms and T-shirts took their place. My mind seemed to be in a constant whirl, I began to feel imprisoned at work. Jennie had the skills and the knowledge of the sector, whereas I simply had the stress of meeting the payroll. I felt like I was playing second fiddle, that my contribution wasn't helping anyone and quite frankly I wished I wasn't there.

Of course, half of me wasn't there anyway. I was beginning to sleep more and more during the day. At times it would seem that I would sit down and immediately fall asleep. When I woke up in the morning, I would instantly feel tired. I thought that it was my feelings about work that were causing my lethargy, but in reality it was something a lot more serious. Something that wouldn't be picked up by the doctors until before the operation, still some years ahead. On one frightening occasion, I was driving into work with Jennie when the traffic lights ahead of us turned red. When they turned green again, we continued to sit there. Jennie turned to me to tell me that the lights had changed and to ask what on earth I was doing. Of course, I was sitting in the driver's seat fast sleep. This had fortunately never happened before (and even more fortunately has never happened since). On another occasion, we were having a meeting with some of our senior staff and someone turned to speak to me only to discover that I was sound asleep. Such instances were highly embarrassing. As someone who always prided myself on my business drive and determination, I was becoming a shadow of my previous self.

I did manage to achieve one feat in attempting to lose the weight. I stopped drinking Coke. I went from drinking four or five litres a day to nothing. I thought that this would really help reduce my weight. After all, I was knocking back over 2,000 calories a day this way. OK, I did replace some of the Coke with other fizzy pop, but certainly not in the sort of quantities I was drinking before. The majority of my fluid intake was now plain old water. It was as though my body was a temple! A pretty big temple, but a temple nonetheless. Unfortunately, this reduction in my sugar intake had no effect on my weight at all. I simply must have eaten more in order to replace what I had cut out. I was really disheartened by this. I thought I had done so well in cutting something out, but had got no reward for it.

I felt that my life was going nowhere. I was in a terrible emotional state, not being bothered about anything at all. I can't believe I lived this way for the two years before my operation. I went to bed, I woke up, ate, went to work, ate, slept, ate, drove home, ate, made dinner, ate, fell asleep in front of the television and then repeated the process again. Oh, I forgot going to the toilet. I went to the toilet a lot. It was probably the most exercise I got. About three or four visits a day – I guess the food I consumed had to go somewhere! And I was getting too fat to fit on it. At home we had to take the seat off so I could fit myself on. I would dread having to visit family and friends, simply because using the loo was a nightmare. Afterwards, cleaning up was also becoming a problem. I simply couldn't easily get my arm round the back. My dignity was fading fast.

Soon this took a further turn for the worse when I realised that I would also have to pee sitting down. My weight had become so much of an issue that finding the 'equipment' to pee out of was also a major hassle. The fat build-up had simply become too much in that area which resulted in me pretty much standing up and spraying everywhere. Basically, there was no other option but to complete the task sitting down.

Worse was to come when we went on a boating holiday to Ireland with a couple of our friends. We hired a big boat and spent two weeks cruising up and down the Shannon, but I was now too fat to fit through the door of the toilet! So I was left having to pee in a cut-off lemonade bottle at night and then having to stop at all the riverside loos during the day. The good thing about the holiday, though, was that all the fresh air actually kept me awake. There was no danger of falling asleep. It was amazing how many hours were in a normal day. Of course, in a moment of madness, we did manage to run the boat aground. We had to get pulled off the rocks but fortunately avoided doing a *Titanic*. I found myself not able to do the things that I wanted to because I simply couldn't walk anywhere. Whenever I even stood up, it generated such a pressure on my back that I had to lean just to take the pressure off my spine.

After returning home from this trip, I began to think with some seriousness about weight-loss surgery. I did some research on the Internet and was forced to concede that, though it was a drastic and potentially dangerous procedure, the results were frequently compelling. People had certainly had some incredible successes, and reading about how lives were improved after surgery made a big impact on me. I saw that there were two basic types, a band and a bypass. The bypass really didn't appeal to me at all. It involved the rerouting of your plumbing which was a change that the patient had to live with for the rest of their life. I didn't fancy the prospect of my food choices being permanently restricted. There was something in my mind that was somehow offended by this thought. I did however warm to the idea of getting a band fitted – it seemed to be a quick operation, and it could always be reversed once I had lost the weight. I assumed that I would only have about 10 or 12 stone to lose, so I thought that this was going to be the best option. I sat on this idea a while, mulling it over in my mind. What I should have done was go to the doctor to get the process moving.

I also thought about going to the doctor about my sleeping problem, but Jennie kept on telling me that it was simply because I was fat. Which was right, it was because I was fat, but it still needed sorting out. But, as with going to the doctor to see about the weight-loss surgery, I put this off as well. At night my snoring was so bad that poor Jennie couldn't get any sleep, which in turn meant that she became ratty with me. Some nights I tried on purpose not to go to sleep so I wouldn't annoy her. I felt Jennie was being a little bit harsh with me. It wasn't the first time that her frustration at my condition made itself clear. I understood where she was coming from and I was petrified that I was going to lose her.

My life drifted aimlessly for a while and every week I spent mulling over visiting the doctor about the operation was a week when I was getting bigger and bigger. You know it is getting bad when the Chinese-takeaway man asks if you want your usual order or the pizza-delivery boy starts sending you birthday cards! I had to cancel a business appointment because I was simply too fat to fit into any smart clothing. I was now letting business fall through my fingers because I couldn't go to a meeting and give a favourable, professional impression.

I finally went to see my GP to discuss getting an appointment to see a specialist about weight-loss surgery. He was just as brilliant about my weight as he had always been. He said he'd put my details down in a letter to the Primary Care Trust (PCT) and we would have to go through a long process of getting approval for the procedure. I was a bit disappointed that I wouldn't be going to see someone quickly but at least the ball was rolling and maybe there was light at the end of the tunnel.

The wait was far longer than I ever imagined. Getting approval for this type of thing was full of yards and yards of red tape. And the longer I waited, the more I ate and the more my weight increased. How much I weighed at this stage I can only imagine. But I know that now I moved into 8XL clothing. I couldn't afford to go any higher – the clothing simply didn't come in a bigger size! My path was following the same route as any person with an addiction. I needed more and more of my drug in order to get my fix. My weight was increasing quicker and quicker, compounding my problems. I was so desperately unhappy, I could see that if something didn't happen quickly then I'd be bed-bound within a year or two and then I'd be faced with problems beyond my imagination. The thought of suicide did cross my mind occasionally. I thought that everyone would be better off without me. Jennie would be free to go and find a new man, a man that could give her everything she wanted. After all, I was simply unable to do so. I was killing myself slowly, so why not simply get the whole process done and dusted quicker, I reasoned, and then everyone could simply get on with their lives. If I did end it all, then we could get the JCB in to bury me, like I had always joked. But suicide, along with everything else, was simply one more thing that, in the end, I couldn't be bothered to go through.

That summer was a nightmare. I was constantly hot. Hot equated to one thing: sweat! I don't think that I'm revealing a state secret when I say that fat men sweat. They actually sweat a lot. This led to a lot of nasty problems. Firstly, the obvious one: it didn't look good and it didn't smell good. My shirt was often soaked in sweat which compounded my not insignificant embarrassment. When people stopped to stare at me, which they did all the time, this just made things worse. But the sweat also caused other problems. I'd get terrible boils between my legs and on my groin. These would cause me pain and when they burst they left nasty stains on my clothing. Also the sweat would cause horrifically painful sores and rashes under my belly, where it overhung my waist. At times it was so painful it was like being cut in two with a sword. I tried to make sure that I showered every single morning, but even this wasn't enough. I really needed to shower two or three times a day to ensure that I was clean. I simply didn't have the energy for this and opted to use cream to calm down the redness and soreness.

It was the time of year that I always go with my father and Siobhan to the Test Match. I love cricket and the trip to the Oval once a year is normally a highlight. But the previous year, I had found it a massive struggle. As opposed to getting the Tube, I would have had to get a cab, simply because I couldn't manage the walk from the ticket office to the platform. However, at the end of the match the previous year, I couldn't get a cab for love nor money. I waited for the crowds to clear, leaning on a wall puffing and blowing like a 90-year-old man. It took me an hour to edge my way on to the Tube at the Oval – I was a walking target for a mugging. Of course, this is only the travelling arrangements to and from the ground. At the ground itself, I'd have great problems with the seating.

Seating seems to be the bane of my life. Wherever I go, I have to think about what the seating is going to be like. I dread going to people's houses in case I break the chairs. I simply can't go to restaurants if the chairs have arms. I hadn't been to the cinema for two years because the seats wouldn't take my weight let alone my width. But all of these things pale in comparison to the seating at a cricket ground. They're cheap, they're plastic and they're small. They're designed to get as many fans as possible into the ground and then ensure that they are in maximum discomfort so that they're always having to visit the bar to get some feeling back in their buttocks. Now, if these seats are bad for a normal person, they are like hell on earth for me. In fact, normally we move ourselves into an area with a slightly restricted view because they aren't actually sold and I can enjoy the 'luxury' of two seats side by side.

This year I was dreading the whole experience. If I had found the previous year a struggle, then what was going to happen this year, I wondered, especially as I had piled on yet more weight. I'd been panicking about it for weeks. I simply didn't want to go. Actually if I was honest, I'd have to admit to myself that I physically couldn't go. But breaking that news to Dad was another matter, as he had spent a lot of money on the tickets and he loved his cricket more than me. He, like most people, also didn't really understand what I was physically and emotionally going through. I worked myself up into such a state that an hour before I was supposed to leave to go to the station I was in floods of tears rocking back and forth on the bed at home, muttering, 'I can't do it, I can't do it.' Jennie was forced to ring my dad and explain that I was in no state to go. He was very understanding, as he normally is. But I couldn't help but feel that I had let him down.

In fact I was feeling that I was letting everyone down. My performance at work was appalling, I was basically going in simply to sleep. In the past, I had been full of energy and ideas, but quite frankly I couldn't have cared less any more. I was being carried and it must have been very heavy work. I felt I was letting down Jodie – I couldn't keep my eyes open long enough to help her with homework. She never said, but it was clear that she was very embarrassed by me. Who wouldn't be? I was embarrassing myself.

After all of this time, my sofa at home had developed a massively deep hole in it where I sat, slept and ate. It was as though this hole was coming to swallow me up completely. Life as I had known it had evaporated. I was barely able to move, I spent most of my time asleep and when I was awake I had no energy, no drive and no real care about what was happening to me. Quite frankly I was a waste of space and not worthy of the life I had been given.

Then the letter with the details of my appointment at St Richard's arrived. And everything, just everything was going to change!

3 March 2009

One day to go! Doesn't time fly when you're enjoying yourself!

By this stage I just want to get it all over and done with.

It's fair to say that I'm finding moving about a little bit easier at the moment. I must have lost over a stone since starting the milk diet. Just think, in six months, I could well have lost almost ten stone, what a transformation that could be.

There is no point in worrying any more. It's all going to happen so I may as well be relaxed about it.

The tension is very heavy in the air. Jennie and I know this could be the last day we spend together, but, typically for us, nothing is spoken.

In fact, we had a busy day. I had agreed to pose for some pictures for a photographer who is doing an obesity exhibition. So we spent two or three hours doing that. The entire house was set up with full lighting – the guy had an assistant and everything. It all felt a bit seedy, me posing in my undercrackers. I should have thought about this a while ago. I bet there is a 'specialist' market who would pay a fortune for this sort of thing. I could have been the world's fattest porn star!

But the photo shoot passed the day and at least we weren't just forced to sit watching the clock and in apprehensive silence.

I go downstairs and write some words for Jennie in case I don't come back. Of course, it's difficult and the notepaper soon becomes damp with tears. I try to end with a joke, but not sure if I manage it.

I just pray she doesn't need to read them.

No doubt sleep is going to be impossible, but I

turn in at ten. My bag already packed. As I have to be there at 7.30am it's going to be one hell of an early start.

Tomorrow I either regain my life or... well, let's not think about that.

My Darling Jennie,

If you are reading this, then things didn't work out quite as we had hoped.

I just wanted to put down a few thoughts for you.

I'm ashamed that things fell apart so badly over the last few years. I'll always feel guilty that I wasn't the husband that I always wanted to be and, more importantly, the husband that you deserved. I never wanted to be such a burden. I'm so sorry that I wasn't able to put matters right before we had to part.

But there were good times, lots of them, please remember them.

You were my friend, my companion, my soul mate – I'll still be thinking the end of your sentences from wherever I am looking over you. And I will be looking over you, trying my best to keep you safe. I'll never really be parted from you. I'll always be there.

I gave you words from good old Fred on our wedding day and I'll leave you for now with these words – Freddie probably wrote them for an occasion like this.

Love of my life don't leave me,
You've stolen my love and now desert me,
Love of my life can't you see,
Bring it back bring it back,
Don't take it away from me,
Because you don't know what it means to me

I've got to go because the paper is getting wet now. If you want just talk to me then I promise I'll be listening.

Stay strong for Jodie.

Forever.

Neil

X

P.S. If you really want to get the JCB I won't mind. Now smile!

13

OPERATION DAY

O-Day. The countdown has finally ended. I feel remarkably relaxed; Jennie, on the other hand, is a walking ball of tension – she tries hard to put on a brave and calm face, but I know better. Up at 5am and had a good old shower, a necessary requirement before the operation.

Hitting the road in the car, it soon becomes apparent that my legendary skill of arriving at an appointment some two hours before I am due has left me. The sat nav informs me that we won't arrive at St Richard's till 7.45am, some 15 minutes late. This is a problem as I know I'm first on the list and the last thing I want is to be bumped down. So consequently I drive like Lewis Hamilton, within the national speed limit of course. This turns out to be a good thing, instead of thinking about the operation I'm concentrating on keeping the car on the road.

I claw back the time and we arrive at the hospital five minutes early, only to find the car park closest to the entrance closed for seemingly no reason. Consequently I have to park round the other side of the hospital with a walk ahead of me. I covered the distance pretty quickly for a 43-stone bloke. The advantage of this was the oxygen and blood really got pumping around my body, just as the medical team like. I'm not sure if they wanted my heart to be trying to break its way out of my chest, though.

We meet a sound guy from the film crew in the lift. The camera man had been waiting for me at the main entrance, but due to the car parking I sneaked in through the back entrance. The director was late, stuck on a ferry from the Isle of Wight.

We check in to the Alwick Bay. I see one person from the assessment day and another lady is in the bed opposite me. Everyone is good natured and very supportive of one another. The next half-hour is a bit of a whirlwind with the film crew taking shots and the nurses doing blood pressure, oxygen and filling in a million and one forms. This is all good because there is no time to think about anything. The anaesthetist arrives for a quick chat – he's one of the key men who is going to keep me alive this morning, so he's a guy I need to keep on the right side of. He seems happy with everything and says he will see me shortly.

It's weighing-in time. Time to see just how many

pounds have been shed on the ten days of the milk diet. The scales show a 14kg weight loss down from 272 to 258 (can't fault my maths even on a stressful morning). This is just shy of 2.5 stone. Pretty impressive over such a short period, I'd say. I wonder if there is any way of living on the milk diet for the next six months and skipping the operation? No, maybe not. Everyone seems pretty pleased with this weight loss – no one more so than me. I've actually felt a difference in the days leading up to the op. Going up the stairs was far easier and there was no need to potter up there like a little old lady, I was going up one step at a time and not the two-footed approach.

Shaw Somers, the surgeon who is about to change my life, appears dressed impeccably in a suit. He has such a calm and reassuring nature and presence that I can't help but feel that I'm in the best possible hands. Yet mistakes do happen. Shaw has a little chat with me to allay my nerves, and says because I've done so well on the milk diet he would be prepared to do the operation by laparoscopic (keyhole) surgery as opposed to standard open surgery. Basically, this means he will do the operation via six pencil-sized holes across the stomach. It's unbelievable to think that he will be able to rearrange my internal organs via this method. One of the advantages of this procedure is that the recovery time is quicker so I could be out of hospital a day sooner.

On the negative side, the gall bladder can't be removed. Gall stones are a common problem during rapid weight loss, which hopefully will happen, and so may mean further surgery to correct this if my body produces them. Also on the negative side, the risk of complications such as bleeding is slightly highly with this method. After a short discussion with Jennie, we decide to go for the keyhole. Any way of being able to get out of hospital quicker is going to win brownie points with me.

We weren't to know at the time the complications that would occur.

We then had to repeat the entire performance for the benefit of the film cameras – twice! I ended with a final flourish by signing the consent form. Shaw disappeared to scrub up. I hoped he'd had an early night and was fighting fit; my life after all was in his hands.

More questions from the TV people regarding how me and Jennie were feeling. I just echoed how excited I felt and how keen I was to get it all over and done with. Jennie was very good. I could see her welling up but she promised me she wouldn't cry in front of me and she was as good as her word.

And then the time was upon us. A short walk down to theatre in my very attractive gown. I did manage to get down there without my arse falling out the back, which was some achievement. What struck me were the number of procedures in place to ensure no cock-ups. The nurse from the ward handed me over to the theatre team and I had to go through the same questions for a second time that morning. And I again confirmed that it was my signature on the consent form – there would be no room for blame if things went wrong.

Jennie was distraught at having to leave, but again she held it together till she turned away from me. I could tell she was in tears. I really felt for her, the last thing I want to do is upset my wife. I was lucky that I had the easy job: all I had to do was lie there and go to sleep; she, however, had all the waiting around to contend with. It mustn't be easy waiting for a loved one while he has an operation that might kill him. This is something I'm going to dread if we manage to get Jennie booked in for surgery as well.

The theatre nurse took me through to the theatre itself. It's amazing how many people they can get in one room. Chris is wandering about with his camera, making sure he films me from all bloody angles. The anaesthetist gets me on the table, which seems very small for a super morbidly obese person and gets me settled. Two inflatable cuffs go round the calf muscles to try to reduce the risk of deep vein thrombosis, another problem linked to obesity and lack of movement. The anaesthetist keeps up a constant stream of banter as he begins sticking things in me. Unfortunately, as I fear, he can't find my artery – always a problem when it comes to me giving blood (and very ironic with what is to come). It took a while but after fiddling around with both wrists he found it. There was no pain, nothing like the horrendous series of blood tests during the sleep assessment. He sends through a little of a drug designed to enable them to monitor my Sats (ie the percentage of oxygen in my blood) before knocking me out. He says I will feel a little drowsy, but it has little effect on me. The Sats were reading 95 per cent so that was pretty good.

A few seconds later, the anaesthetic was administered and I was out like a light.

The gastric bypass operation went like a dream (well, certainly for me!) and was completed in just over 11/2 hours. There was, however, one small complication, the chances of which were 1 in 1,000. When one of the scopes entered my body, a blood vessel was nicked in my stomach. It's not good to nick a blood vessel at the best of times but, when it's deep under inches and inches of fat, it's even worse. Obviously the bleeding has to be stopped but it's difficult to see where it is. Shaw devised an interesting solution to the problem by inserting a catheter into the stomach and pumping up the balloon in order to apply pressure on the wound to stop the flow of blood. After 11/4 hours, the loss of blood was finally stopped.

The operation lasted far longer than anyone expected. Jennie did her best to wear a hole in the hospital floor, with her constant pacing up and down. She was driving the nurses mad, asking them if there was any news from the theatre. Finally she got the news that everything was OK and I was just waking up. 'Fine,' she said, 'not that I was panicking at all!'

The first thing I remember is waking up in recovery with a massive pain in my left shoulder. I don't have a clue where I am or what I am doing there. As I slowly begin to come to my senses, I feel massively nauseous and an injection is given to prevent any further vomiting, not that there was anything in my system of course. From my bed I can see a clock. 3pm. I went down to theatre at 9am so it is pretty clear to me that something isn't quite right. The nurse who never moved more than an inch from the foot of the bed explained about the bleed and that I was about to be moved into the High Dependency Unit. The words High Dependency have a certain ring to them, and not an altogether pleasant one.

The pain in my shoulder starts to ease a little in HDU. A nurse called Zoe never strayed more than half a foot from my bed. She records my heart rate, Sats, blood pressure and respiration rates into a big chart at regular intervals. This I know is the critical time; the riskiest period is immediately following the operation. People who have died have suffered massive heart failures from the result of the anaesthetic. Jennie and Siobhan are allowed to visit me and you could really see the relief on their faces when they see me awake. The constant beeping of the machines is worrying me. Being one of life's constant worriers, a HDU is probably not the best place to be. It is soon made clear that the only reason I am on the HDU ward is because of the bleed and it is purely as a precautionary measure – so I manage to relax a little.

Suddenly, I'm presented with an hour of pure comedy genius. It's time for me to get out of bed and move to a chair. Mobilisation of obese patients is critical in order to prevent pressure sores and DVTs. I was told prior to the operation that I would be out of bed between four and six hours after coming round. This is, of course, if the staff could get the bed to work. The beds on the bariatric ward are naturally designed for the task in hand. My bed for example could handle weights of up to 350kg – that's even fatter than me! The beds are so clever they can move in about a thousand and one different directions. Since arriving in the HDU ward, I've been stuck quite some distance in the air as it makes things easier for the nurses when doing stuff to you. And they can't actually get the bed to go down so I can get out. One of the staff nurses on HDU – I'll call him Hugo, not his real name – really can't seem to understand it and within a short period there are five nurses around the bed all pressing buttons, plugging things in and then unplugging the same things. After much effort, they manage to get the feet area to go down and, with a little careful manoeuvring, I get myself into the fat chair at the side of my bed.

I am surprised at the lack of any real pain in the abdominal area. I was expecting that first movement to be agony but it wasn't the case. I am of course fuelled by morphine so maybe this has some kind of dulling effect. While I sit in the chair with Jennie next to me, Hugo is on the phone – to the bed company. It's 10pm and he's giving some poor little customer-service bloke the roasting of his life. Hugo wants an engineer here and he wants one now. He has a patient (me) who needs to use the bed so Hugo isn't taking no for an answer. By now all the nurses on the HDU ward and the bariatric ward know the saga of the bed. It's the talk of the hospital. In the end, Hugo, who is now off the phone, has another go and, as if by some divine miracle, it works.

Shaw pops his head round the door to check up on me, and he explains the bleed. He too asks about the bed. I'm half-expecting Barack Obama to come on the phone enquiring about the state of my bed. Shaw says that, as things are going fine, I'm going to be moved back into the bariatric ward. This makes me feel better – things have got to be good if you're moving away from HDU.

14
WORRYING TIMES

I really can't praise the level of care I received at the hospital highly enough. But, despite the best efforts of my fantastic medical team, there is nothing like being at home and I couldn't wait to be discharged.

I had been wheeled out of HDU later that same evening and back into the ward where everyone else was recovering. I didn't really get a good night's sleep that night. Everyone's machines kept pinging, my blood pressure and temperature were taken every hour and there was a mad woman who had just had a band fitted and was determined to walk about the ward all night.

I was suffering considerable lower back pain when in bed and after the night following the operation I simply couldn't wait to get out of bed again. My first day was still pretty difficult, I had a catheter in, still had a nasal throat tube and was still linked up to both fluids and morphine. I kept swapping between the chair and the bed, trying to ease the pressure on my spine. It's fair to say that I am probably one of the worst people in the world for getting bored. I have a terribly short attention span and keeping myself occupied was a nightmare. I spent the majority of my time in that age-old gentlemanly pursuit – trying to pass wind.

During the operation, the body is filled with gas in order to help the surgeon do his job. It basically expands everything inside you and ensures that all the organs are as far apart from each other as possible. The only thing is, the gas remains in your system afterwards and really makes you feel uncomfortable. It was this gas that had been giving my shoulder so much pain when I woke up. The only way of getting rid of it is via the two traditional methods – passing wind and burping. The ward was soon a hotbed of methane activity. Unfortunately, it wasn't me that was producing it, it was my companions. No matter how hard I tried, I couldn't get rid of any, which left me feeling very uncomfortable and slightly hesitant, wondering if everything had been sewn up properly again.

The mad woman was driving everyone, well, let's see – mad. She was complaining to the poor nursing staff about everything.

As for me, I started on fluids proper on day one, which was fantastic. All night I had been allowed to suck the end of a small sponge which had been put in water – it wetted the mouth but that was about it. Today I could drink water, one very small glass of fruit juice every hour. I had to be very careful at this stage because we had to be sure that there were no leaks and that I didn't damage my new tiny tummy by overloading it. As I've said, I have the attention span of a goldfish especially if I am uncomfortable, so I soon decided to start investigating the state of my wounds. I was halfway through poking my fingers down one of the dressings when I was hurriedly told off by one of the nurses. Wounds and dirty fingers equal infection, apparently!

By early afternoon, the wind still wasn't passing. I felt like I wanted to fart and burp simultaneously. Neither was happening. In the meantime, I wasn't short of visitors: Jennie was around of course. She had managed to sweet-talk the nurses on the ward into allowing her to come in all day because she was staying in a little local B&B. And Mum and Pete had also come all the way down from Burton. They were staying overnight in a hotel. But after half an hour or so of talking I got very tired and cat-napped my way through the afternoon. Jennie had bought me a lovely little teddy bear, so with all this attention and care I thought I was five again. Jodie had apparently been on the phone and despite her 'stiff upper lip' she was pretty desperate to see me and prove to herself that I was in fact still in the land of the living. So the following day she was going to come down to the hospital with Siobhan.

I insisted that Jennie go and get an early night, as it had been a pretty stressful 48 hours. Thankfully, the mad woman had been discharged. I think she had been sent away before she was dispatched to the morgue. So I was looking forward to a better night's kip. The nose tube had been removed so my CPAP (continuous positive airway pressure) mask fitted better and wasn't pissing out air at great volumes like it was last night. After the drama of the previous evening, I was able to move the bed up and down a little, so I was able to ease my back a little. God knows why it hurt so much, it was probably simply the position I had been put in after the surgery.

The monitoring was easing off a little now and my blood pressure was taken only a few times that night, which meant I was able to have a much more restful sleep. And I was thrilled to be able to get out of bed at 6am and stretch my legs. I was allowed to drink a bit more that morning and therefore the drip came out and the morphine was removed halfway through the night. It felt good to be a bit freer. Then, joy of joys. The catheter came out and that was heaven – well, not the actual removal which was a little uncomfortable and quite a lot embarrassing.

On the third day, it was time to eat! Food – I'd

forgotten what it was. It was almost a fortnight since I had actually eaten anything. It was amazing: I was truly not bothered about it any more. It was like I had gone through cold turkey with the milk diet – completely abstaining from my addiction. Going down the hospital menu and choosing the meals for the day was quite a novel experience, deciding what to eat again. Of course, the selection wasn't quite what I was used to; there were no T-bone steaks and certainly no chips. For breakfast, I had a small amount of yogurt. And I mean a *small* amount. I managed practically a thimble full before I simply had eaten enough. Unbelievable. All those years of wanting more and more, always thinking about where the next meal was coming from and now, just like that, the craving, the desire and most importantly the capability were gone.

Being free of wires was excellent and I pottered about a little bit. With Jennie's help, I managed to have a shower, which was really needed for washing under my belly. It was sweaty and very smelly down there. There was a moment of drama when I slipped and almost fell. I got into a set of pyjamas, which was far better than my very attractive operating gown. My dressings were changed and I got the first look at my wounds. It was amazing how small they were, just astonishing that, for such a significant change inside my body, this was all I had to show for it. Shaw did his rounds and wanted to have a good look at my wounds, especially the big one. He was pleased at how they were healing and I hoped that I would be allowed home the following day. He said he would see how things went.

I went for a pee on the loo – it was a shock after the catheter that I had to think about that again. And what a relief – I managed to let loose a massive fart. Good God, did it feel good! I let out a little squeal of joy. Then I started on the peppermint tea which aided burping. I was in farting and burping heaven and didn't care in the slightest who heard.

Lunchtime came and I had some tuna mayonnaise. I probably managed about two or three cola-bottle-tops full. But I have to admit it did taste good. I used the smallest possible fork and just put a very small amount into my mouth. I had another round of visitors and this time I was a bit more lively. I think Jodie was pleased to see me, although you wouldn't have thought it. Jennie disappeared for her tea down the canteen and left her Fanta on my table. The nurses went into a panic thinking I'd been drinking it. No, I assured them, it was my wife's and I hadn't even been remotely tempted by it. For tea, I had a dish of puréed fruit with some cream. It was still important that I ate fat, because fat is actually one of things that the body needs in order to function correctly.

At bedtime, I even found myself declining a Rich Tea

biscuit. I simply didn't want to eat. I was hoping that tomorrow I would be allowed home. I have to say it was now getting pretty boring. I just wanted to get back, recover and get on with the rest of my life.

The next day I was waiting impatiently for Shaw to come round to tell me I could go home. He had another day of surgery ahead; they didn't mess about in here. It was like a production line. While I waited for Shaw, the catheter in the wound was removed – it was a struggle and apart from my back it was the only moment of real pain that I suffered.

Unfortunately, when Shaw came round, he had bad news. Because I'd suffered the complication of minor internal bleeding during the operation, he wanted me to stay an additional night in hospital. I tried to persuade him otherwise. But as we lived so far away he made me stay, and quite rightly so. If anything had gone wrong, I would have been in trouble. After all, I couldn't jump in the car and drive myself back because I wouldn't be able to drive now for a fortnight. I was a little disappointed, but he promised me that he would do my discharge letter and I would be able to leave very first thing in the morning.

Siobhan kindly drove down at 8.30am the next day to pick me up. I just couldn't wait to get back home. Jennie was in early and then, after a round of goodbyes to the nursing staff and my fellow patients, I was off!

It was nice to be back. I hadn't been 100 per cent sure that I would see my house again. Siobhan had very cleverly worked out a great system for me. She had made mashed potatoes and mashed swede and had put it into ice-cube racks in the freezer. So when I wanted a meal all I would have to do was pop one of those out and bung it in the microwave. Cheesy mash became a favourite meal as it gave me the two things I really needed: protein and dairy. My diet had to be high in these things now. Protein was needed for recovery and muscle retention and calcium was needed to keep my bones strong. The only problem I found about being back home was having the courage to lie flat on my broken bed. The beds in the hospital had been on an incline and I felt I was stretching my stomach a little bit too much when completely flat.

Siobhan left for a well-deserved holiday to Spain the next day and I settled down with my recovery. It now took a lot of thought about what to eat because I had to make sure I got the protein in and obviously I didn't want to do any damage to myself. For breakfast I set about tackling a Müller Light. That one small yogurt pot lasted me three breakfasts! Come lunchtime, cheese and biscuits entered the equation. Those first days just one cracker was sufficient. I was also having to think about trying to be mobile and kept going for little walks around the house. It was essential so I didn't develop a

DVT. Jennie had to give me daily injections in the stomach to thin the blood to further reduce the risk.

The third day at home I woke up wanting the loo. I had been in hospital but obviously, with the tiny quantity of food I was eating, there wasn't a great requirement to go regularly. So I crawled out of bed, being careful not to stretch my dressings. I saw a lot of blood on the toilet paper. I looked into the bowl and saw both fresh blood and a lot of dried blood. Passing blood is never good, especially when you've just had an operation on your digestive system and one of the complications was a bleed.

I went and lay back on the bed, trying to convince myself that it was just a pile or that I had burst a vessel. But when I got up again in a few hours I saw the sheets were splattered with blood. Jennie did a not-so-pleasant investigation and, yes, there was still fresh blood dripping out of my bottom! We left it another couple of hours just to see if things would dry up but after that time my tracksuit bottoms were all covered in blood. Jennie rang the ward to ask about it. The result was simple. Get to A & E – quick!

15

A WALK IN THE WOODS

'I'm bleeding out of my rectum.'

Not really the thing you want to tell someone – especially when you've never met the other person before. Even more so when the reception desk at A & E is about five yards from 20-odd people, all of whom have ailments, but who have nothing wrong with their hearing.

In contrast to my positive NHS experience a few days before, the A & E staff were clearly flat out and I feared that I could have quite easily bled to death in the corner. I don't think anyone would have batted an eyelid, though. In a matter of days, I had seen both sides to the British healthcare system. I'd seen the good stuff; now for the ugly side. Of course, this wasn't Chichester and the big panic was that the medical staff here wouldn't understand the kind of procedure I had undergone.

To be fair, once I was seen, I felt in safe hands. It was a shame that, after we had been waiting for four hours, Jennie had to resort to the 'my husband's just had a serious operation' routine. I've never had my 'areas' investigated before and, to put it mildly, it wasn't the most comfortable feeling in the world, especially as I was lying on my side on a very small examination table. So I was trying my best not to fall off as the doctor pushed his forefinger around inside me.

Thankfully, he immediately ruled out anything to do with the operation, which was a massive relief. I really didn't need any complications now. He thought that I had a very big pile, one that might well need to be surgically removed. I felt despair – another operation! Within seven days of the last one, and by people who weren't specially trained in caring for the super morbidly obese – I didn't think so. However, I was lucky, as there was a surgical specialist in the vicinity who could have a quick look. Five minutes later, I had two blokes probing about up there. It turned out it wasn't a pile, it was a sort of blood clot which had formed because of sitting on hard surfaces. That bloody hospital bed and the hard bariatric chairs on the ward immediately leaped to my mind. The specialist decided he wouldn't mess about, no need to come in for any surgery. A bit of heavy-handed squeezing, 30 seconds with a little pair of scissors and a lot of sweat and yelping from me, and the problem was solved and my bottom was being padded out with a lot of cotton-wool dressings.

It was a relief to know that nothing was wrong. The panic I felt when the thing wouldn't stop bleeding was horrendous. Setbacks are not uncommon with my type of surgery and I'd had enough of them just thinking about the possibility that something bad could happen. I was determined that in reality I wasn't going to have any.

Four days after going home, the dressings came off the wounds. All that remained were the strips left holding the wounds together. Apart from the indent that was still present in the biggest wound, everything seemed to be healing very nicely indeed. Each scar was less than an inch long, truly remarkable for such a complex piece of surgery. Now the dressings were off, I could enjoy a decent shower. The strips would slowly dissolve over the next few weeks. I was very careful in the shower taking extreme care not to slip; I certainly didn't want to fall and break something.

Finding things to eat was very difficult. I'd been given guidance sheets from the hospital which recommended lots of soups and liquidised foods – not things that I really liked. I managed some chicken soup but couldn't bring myself to try anything liquidised, it would be like eating baby food, and I had a lifelong aversion to sauces and anything that made my food wet. So I lived off cheese and biscuits, yogurts and cheesy mash for a while. Not the most exciting of diets but at least things I could eat. The volume I was eating was pitiful. Not really enough to fill a bird, but of course this was the whole point of the exercise – a massive reduction in calories. Oddly, I found I wasn't really missing eating. More than anything, it became a task, something that had to be done, but not something that I would necessarily choose to do.

I was fortunate, many people are often very sick after the op because the new stomach struggles to cope with food again. I didn't have any of that, but then I was extremely careful, even frightened of eating. Whenever I felt something funny happening down there, I simply stopped eating.

I wasn't back at work yet, but there is only so much horse-racing and so many reruns of *Only Fools and Horses* that a man can watch before he gets bored. I was finding it hard to fill my day, mainly because my day was so long now that the CPAP machine was doing so well in helping me enjoy decent, uninterrupted sleep at night. I never felt tired and never wanted a nap during the day. I got up at 7am and went to bed at 11pm or midnight with a good solid sleep in between. Looking back, it was terrible to think how much of my life had been lost over the last few years simply by being asleep. I didn't want to have to sleep with the machine for the rest of my life, as sounding like Darth Vader isn't the greatest turn-on in the world. Unless you like a lot of black leather, I suppose! I wondered how much weight I would have to lose before I could bid goodbye to the CPAP machine.

The one thing I wasn't doing was exercise. I needed to take the plunge and get out and do something more than walking around in circles in the lounge. So Jennie and I decided to go for a little walk in the woods behind the house. Now it's safe to say I hadn't been for anything that could have been classed as a walk for years, apart from the charge along the hospital corridors on the morning of the operation. The plan was to walk to the bridge over the little stream which was about 500 yards into the woodland. Not very far, but far enough to get the blood flowing and the heart pumping a little bit. It was a beautiful day, the sun was shining and the daffodils were out in full force. The birds were singing in the trees which were just starting to blossom and it was a wonderful spring afternoon. Buster, our cocker spaniel, loved the walk – the poor little fella hadn't really got out much recently, which was a shame as he really enjoys it. Hopefully, I'd be able to take him out a bit more and get a bit of weight off him as well – this operation was going to be good for everyone, pets included, I said to myself. The woods had really changed since the last time I had been in, which must have been about three years previously. The pathway was clear, whereas last time it was very overgrown, although it was still very uneven. I was very careful with my footing, I didn't want to come crashing to the ground and injure myself. It would be just my luck that I'd get through the operation and then suffer a broken leg, I thought!

I found the walk no problem at all, although it was more of a gentle staggering. A nice sedate pace with the sun on your face and it's unbelievable what can be achieved. I got to the bridge in one go and without getting out of breath. Jennie and I stood and watched the fish swim in the stream from the bridge and had a little kiss. It was perfect. I was a little bit tired coming back and was glad of the dining-room chair as soon as I walked through the door. But I was sitting down with that nice, warm glow you get after doing some exercise. Just those few simple minutes broke the psychological barrier which up to this point told me that I couldn't walk. My freedom was coming back.

Trying to get enough liquids into my body was proving to be a bit of a problem. My normal big gulps of fluid were now a complete and utter no-go. Returning from my walk, I was thirsty. I had been breathing heavily on the way back, through my mouth, which in turn dried the throat. I drank half a glass very quickly and immediately knew something was wrong. There was an immediate feeling of tightness in my upper chest as though I was trying to swallow a brick. It was as though I could feel the water backing up my food pipe and waiting in a queue in order to be able to drip, drop by drop, into my stomach. After a few minutes, the discomfort died away but it was an experience that I vowed I wouldn't be repeating in the near future. I must remember to sip.

Over the next few days, we repeated our stroll through the woods. I even ventured a little further than the bridge. The pace was pretty slow but it didn't matter, I was outside, I was walking and more importantly I was enjoying it. It helped my back which since I had got home from hospital had been a complete nightmare. Any longer than half an hour sitting on the sofa and it would start screaming to me in agony. I couldn't really understand what was behind this but on the positive side at least it was keeping me moving about.

Jennie didn't fancy the walk in the woods one day so I thought I would venture out with Buster on my own. In all the years that I had lived there, I hadn't properly explored the woods so I thought this would be a good opportunity to go a little further and see what was about. It was an interesting area. It had been the site of the old gunpowder mills in the 19th century and the remains of the buildings could still be seen. But what was more interesting was the series of manmade streams that obviously had been used to transport goods back to the main river. These days there were dams and weirs in place in order to keep these streams shallow but the banks were still really steep and showed the size of the boats that must have been in use back then.

The main path followed the top of one of these banks. It was a fair way from the edge so there was no danger of falling over. This is the way I went, Buster charging around on his long lead like a little idiot. Buster can never be let off the lead because he'd just run away and only come back when and if he chose to. Alas, my dog-training skills weren't something I had kept up with, so Buster couldn't be trusted and was restricted to long lead only. I got to the bridge and walked on – I'd continued past this point the other day and was interested to see what was round the corner. So off I went. I was now trying to stride forward with a bit of purpose, as opposed to looking like I was using an invisible zimmer frame. As I rounded the corner, the ground seemed to get a bit more overgrown, the nettles were certainly out in force. I shouted at Buster to slow down and to get a bit closer to me because the ground was becoming uneven and I was having to slow down. Next thing I knew, my foot had gone down a rabbit hole and I found myself lying flat on my back halfway down a 10ft slope midway between the path and the stream.

I was in trouble here and I knew it. Nothing seemed to be broken but I was very shaken up and was missing both my shoe and my dog. My first thought was to get the dog. He'd more than likely be halfway to Glasgow now. I shouted to him and as if by a miracle he appeared – no doubt to see why my voice had gone all weak and pathetic. He seemed very interested in why I was lying head-first down a steep bank, he clearly thought it was a big game and came down to see me. So now I was lying on a slope with a stream beneath me, with my feet a good four feet above my head, in a massive bed of nettles, one foot without shoe or sock, and a cocker spaniel licking my face. Brilliant! Well done, Neil. How on earth did you manage that one? I thought.

So I'd got the dog and now I had to find my trainer. My foot and calf were going bright red having been stung to almighty hell by the nettles, so this became a matter of urgency. I cursed myself for not having any socks on. Over the previous 12 months or so, I had rarely worn socks because my lower legs and feet were so swollen. I just couldn't find any socks big enough, so I'd stopped using them, something I was completely regretting now. I saw the offending trainer sticking out the top of the rabbit hole, nicely out of my reach.

My problem was that I couldn't get back up. I was completely in the wrong position, literally lying down in a bed of nettles and if I put my hands on the ground to try to push myself up they were going to get as badly stung as my feet. If the situation wasn't so comical I might have been frightened. It was just starting to turn to dusk, and I had no mobile phone on me so I couldn't phone Jennie to ask her to come and help me. I thought about shouting for help, but who on earth was going to hear me? I'd have to hope that Jennie was going to realise before long that I was missing; otherwise, it was going to be a very long, cold night. There I was, no more than 600 yards from home and I had visions of the mountain rescue being called out to find me and then the fire brigade to winch me up – I thought I'd be ending up in the *Daily Mail* after all.

16

LITTLE CHANGES

After spending about ten minutes calming down and reasoning that, as I wasn't in the mountains of British Columbia, I wasn't likely to freeze to death or be ravaged by a hungry bear. I determined that with a little application I was able to solve this unfortunate situation myself. It really wouldn't be good for my recovery to be lying on a wet bank for the next couple of hours, so it was time to go into Bear Grylls mode.

I managed to swing myself round so that my feet were now below my head, which was a far more realistic position to pull myself to my feet. I was still missing my trainer and it wouldn't have been wise to try to get up on a heavily nettled, woodland floor with a bare foot. Fortunately, there was a big stick within easy reach and after five minutes of playing 'hook a duck' I got the offending piece of footwear back. It was somewhat painful putting the thing back on because by now my foot was covered in those awful white bumps you get when you've been stung by nettles. By now, I had that god-awful tingly feeling, that is almost pins and needles, but not quite. I did the laces up as tight as they would go, to ensure no further footwear malfunction. My failure to do this in the first place is why the thing came off so easily, and as my feet were so swollen it was actually very difficult to tie any piece of footwear up. Well, I say 'any piece' of footwear, these were the only things that I could still actually get on, my normal smart black shoes had long since been relegated to the cupboard under the stairs. So my feet were sorted, but I wasn't in the sort of physical condition to be able to leap up from the ground without putting my hands on the ground and pushing up.

This presented another problem. I had fallen into the biggest area of nettles I had ever seen and, in order to stand up, I would have had to submerge my hands in them to gain purchase on the steep slope. As my hands were already partly stung from the fall, this wasn't something that I was keen on doing. I had a brainwave and stripped off my T-shirt to protect my hands as I stood up. Anyone who happened to pass me on the footpath at that moment would have been confronted with the sight of a half-naked fat man with a cocker spaniel messing about in a bed of nettles. Fortunately, no one appeared and my pride wasn't damaged any further. The T-shirt plan worked nicely and I was soon back on my feet, and after a bit of a scramble I was up the bank and back on the footpath. By this time it was almost completely dark and the ankle that had gone down the hole was stiffening up nicely. I began to stumble back towards home, taking it very slowly and choosing my steps very carefully. As I passed the bridge, I saw a clump of dock leaves down by the stream, ideal for soothing the stings, but I decided that caution is the better part of valour and resisted the urge to retrieve some.

The sympathy I received at home was limited to being called a bumbling fool and being told I wasn't allowed out on my own again. This incident certainly knocked my confidence a bit and unfortunately it also triggered the onset of an old problem – gout in my ankle. Gout is something that I would normally associate with heavy drinkers but I am practically teetotal and a martyr to it. I first got a bout of it five or six years ago. It is a hereditary thing which both my father and my grandfather suffered from. Without going into a long medical explanation, uric acid builds up in the blood and turns into crystals in the joints which in turn then causes pain – a lot of bloody pain. The first time I knew I was suffering from gout, it was in my big toe and I remember screaming when the cat brushed her tail against my toes, such is the agony. As tests showed, I had naturally high uric acid levels; I couldn't really reduce them by a change in diet or a reduction in drinking. In the past, the amount of fluid I would drink would ensure that the acid didn't get a chance to crystallise. Since the operation, the massive reduction in my fluid intake meant that I was at risk of an attack.

Gout comes and goes, with attacks normally lasting a few days and then fading away as if nothing had ever even happened. It was very difficult to put any weight on my foot at all, so any thoughts of doing any exercise vanished. In fact, it was very difficult to even get down the stairs. The whole joint became very stiff, with the pain coming in waves. I could almost feel the blood flowing over the bone, which is the point at which you really want to scream. Jennie wanted me to go and see the doctor, but I really couldn't face taking more pills. I was, after all, finding it very difficult to take the vitamin pill that I had to have every day. You have to take a big gulp of water to wash the thing down and this really hurt. Nothing was less appealing than having to do this three times a day.

This attack was particularly frustrating because I really wanted to pick up the exercise as much as I could. It was such a good feeling to be able to get out of the house, even if it was only for a short walk. There was little that I could do to improve my condition. I couldn't drink a lot to flush the crystals away so I simply had to sit it out. Despite my aversion to pills, I decided to borrow some of the pills that my father took in order to prevent an attack. This surely would be the better course of action, I reasoned. Days passed and nothing happened – if anything, the pain was worse. Finally I relented and went to the doctors.

It was the first time I had driven since the operation and I was a little concerned about braking hard and inflicting damage on myself when the seatbelt tightened. I was advised to leave it a couple of weeks before attempting to get behind the wheel, but when needs must. As I have an automatic car, fortunately the bad foot was not the foot I used for driving, otherwise this process would have been nigh on impossible. The doctor was pleased to see me still alive and duly gave me a few words of wisdom for foolishly taking my father's pills, which had been prescribed to prevent an attack of gout. When you were actually having an attack, these were useless. In fact, they would make the problem worse. Whoops! Big mistake on my part. He prescribed me the correct course of medication and sent me on my way. One pill later and the pain was gone. Fantastic: so easy.

Note to self – don't self-medicate in future!

Following the 'incident' I decided to stay clear of the woods for my walks and instead we followed another path behind the house, which went by the lake. The path was a lot smoother and there were far fewer opportunities for self-inflicted disasters. The smoothness of the path meant that I could try to get a bit of pace going. This way also gave infinite possibilities for the length of walk, as it led into a country park with two further lakes, each with over ten miles of walks around them. Even on this first occasion I managed to get further than I had ever done on this route before. The whole route must have been over at least two miles. I returned home, once more triumphant at my progress.

Two weeks had passed since I had returned home after the operation, so just over a month on the milk diet and already the change in my face was obvious. It is a strange phenomenon of this sort of operation that the weight starts coming off from the top down, a little bit like a Christmas tree. I was wondering how much weight I had now lost, and it was a little frustrating that I couldn't yet weigh myself. I would have to wait until I got my post-op follow-up appointment, to find out – but based on the weight loss on the milk diet I was betting that I had lost another couple of stone. My first target would be to get under that 40-stone barrier, and I was secretly hoping that this might have already happened.

I had returned to work and it was great to get so many positive comments from people about how well I looked. I was still recovering from the operation and did feel tired in the middle of the day, which was to be expected. So I simply went for a little kip. I felt a little bit upset that I needed to sleep during the day. After being on the CPAP machine, I hadn't had to do this for months, so I had to remember that my body was still healing and had gone through a big trauma. It was now also not getting the number of calories that it was used to having in the past, so I guess it was no surprise that I was feeling tired.

The other thing that I had started to notice was that I felt cold all the time. Previously, I couldn't stop myself from sweating, but now I felt cold. It was a case of having to dig out my big fleeces in order to keep warm. Even though it was the middle of spring, my guess was that the amount of food I was eating was so small that the calories from that were being used for vital things as opposed to keeping me warm.

It's funny how you start to pick up on the little changes, like being able to get into the shower more easily. It may not have been long but already these differences were starting to show themselves. The stairs were another thing; I was finding getting up them a lot easier. And I already had to tighten the mask on my CPAP machine because it had become loose on my head.

I'd managed to graduate up to a whole Müller Light for breakfast and was attempting to integrate a few new things into my diet. I had been told that toast often seemed to be tolerated better than bread by bypass patients, so I thought I would give this a try. It was a mistake: it didn't seem to sit very well at all and I only managed a quarter of a slice before giving up. A few days later, there were some croissants in the house which looked fantastic, so I gave one of those a go. I didn't put on any jam because of the sugar content. I was very mindful that sugar was forbidden. It tasted fantastic on its own and kept me full for a good six hours. So the following evening, I decided to have another one before bed. This one also went down very well but then, about 30 seconds later, something clearly wasn't right.

I felt very strange, my chest was very tight and there was a very strange feeling inside the top of my stomach. It wasn't pleasant at all, and I made my way upstairs feeling very rough. I lay on the bed trying to control my breathing. It was as though the food was backing up, waiting to go into my stomach. I knew what was going to happen next and made my way to the bathroom.

I was sick, the first time since the operation – but it was not like being sick prior to the surgery. It was as though I was opening my mouth and tipping myself up so the food would slide out of my stomach. There was a bit of effort involved in this process for really very little gain. Awful. Croissants were struck off my list straight away.

This incident sparked a whole fortnight of sickness. Things that I had eaten in the past without a hitch suddenly didn't agree with me at all. There was no reason to it all. Maybe I was rushing my progress a bit, I don't know, but I knew that many people reported these kinds of problems after the surgery. It was very draining and also a big waste of time – I may as well not have bothered. It got to the stage where I felt like not eating at all, because I didn't want to go through the vomiting.

At times, it was fair to say, I wondered what on earth I had got myself into.

17
WEIGH-IN

For the next month I was still sticking my head down the white porcelain on a regular basis. Things that went down without problem or upset one day disagreed after a single bite the next. Bread still seemed to be a no-go, which wasn't good for lunchtimes at work. So I soon decided to consign bread to the 'do not eat' list. There were also other strange differences: a small corner of a chicken breast, for example, would be fine, whereas a little piece of chicken from the full roast chicken wouldn't be.

There are strict guidance levels regarding food intake that must be followed after undergoing a gastric bypass. Firstly, I have to take a multivitamin pill every single day for the rest of my life. This is because the small intake of food and the reduced absorption of calories and nutrients I'm capable of just isn't sufficient to keep me healthy. Without the multivitamin, my body simply wouldn't get what it needed to function. This in itself caused me a problem in those first few weeks – the pills were so big that I couldn't possibly swallow them whole. I had to try to break the things into three or four pieces with a kitchen knife. Being my normal cack-handed self, I'd send bits of the pills flying in all directions over the kitchen and find myself on my hands and knees groping about under the freezer for my quarter of pill.

Secondly, I have to remember to chew the food I put in my mouth. It sounds basic but looking back I think this was actually a big challenge. I never properly chewed anything, so desperate to get it consumed I'd swallow it back straight away. With such a small opening to my stomach, I had to remember to take small bites in the first place and then chew very well before even thinking about swallowing. This of course made the process of eating very different. It allowed me time to consider what I was actually eating, actually taste the flavours, enjoy the textures and appreciate the whole eating experience.

Thirdly, I have to concentrate on protein. It is vital for bypass patients to make sure that they eat enough protein. Protein is essential for the body to heal itself and also to maintain muscle mass. So this is also the first port of call when choosing foods to eat. It's vital to ensure that you fill up on protein first before starting to eat carbohydrates, to avoid overloading on them. Bizarrely, fruit and vegetables are notoriously difficult to eat post-surgery. Mashed stuff like swede or carrot is fine, but things like tomato skin, apple skin, peaches or any raw vegetables all pose real problems to the recovering patient.

Finally, I had to eat at least three portions of dairy every single day in order to get enough calcium into my system. Calcium, of course, is required to maintain a healthy skeleton. With hopefully becoming a lot more active over the forthcoming years, I needed to ensure that my bones were as strong as they could be.

Bearing these things in mind, there was actually quite a bit of planning that had to go into choosing something to eat. Being at work was the hardest, because I would forget that I needed to take some cheese and crackers or a banana in for lunch. Yes, some days I did just have a banana for lunch. Well, in fact, it would be for morning snack, lunch and then afternoon snack: I would have to eat the thing in three separate sittings (good job I like bananas!). When I forgot lunch, I would be forced to get a tuna sandwich from the van man and then take one or two bites and leave the rest because the bread wasn't agreeing with me. It was one big learning curve and trying to get my mind around the changes was very difficult.

Jennie and I decided one Sunday to broaden our

horizons and drove down to Bewl Water, which is a very large reservoir in Kent. We had visited a few times some years previously, but could never go very far from the car because my walking wasn't up to it. It's a magnificent spot, green woodland and brightly coloured sailing boats on the water. It's a fair walk down a steep bank and then a long set of stairs before you even get down to the edge. We managed a nice two-mile walk in the bracing air and, when we got back, I climbed back to the car without even getting out of breath. Another tick in my triumphs box.

The biggest physical change I had found so far was the diminishing of pain in my back whenever I stood up or when I walked. The strange pain I had when lying down or sitting was still there, but now I seemed to be able to stand up quite freely with no pain in my back whatsoever. This alone could almost have been described as life changing. When you can only stand up straight for about 30 seconds without then having to lean or sit because of pain, this counted as truly liberating.

The next tick in a box came when I ventured down Tonbridge high street. Shops! Amazing things. They have goods inside them that you can purchase with money and take home. Apart from going into a service station or a local supermarket for some 'goodies', I hadn't been into a proper shop for at least three years. The last time I had been on the high street was when we took my father out for his birthday at an all-you-can-eat oriental buffet and I had to risk parking in a disabled spot because I wouldn't have been able to make it from the car park. I was only going to buy a notebook but it was as though I was shopping at Harrods with a blank chequebook.

I was getting very impatient for my letter from the hospital informing me of the post-operative check-up. I thought I would have had it by now and was keen to discuss the vomiting and, of course, find out the magical weight-loss number.

Then my worries about being sick started to subside as I was beginning to recognise my new body more and more. And that is really what it was like – having a whole new body. I was learning to eat, just like a baby. I could detect the feelings that told me to stop eating, or when today wasn't going to be a good day for eating chicken. I learned that chewing was important and something that must be done. I worked out that, if I couldn't eat bread without being sick, then why bother? By learning from these experiences and acting on the signs, I could control my eating patterns and stop myself being sick. And I did. The sickness just went away completely. This was a relief, because you do read horror stories of people whose operations go wrong and the pouch is made too small or they have a blockage or they simply can't tolerate food and then corrections have to be made with further surgery. Fortunately, it seemed, for now, that I was OK.

My letter arrived. The appointment would be just a day short of six weeks after the operation. This time the drive down to St Richard's was a pleasure. After all, there was nothing to worry about at the end of it. Also, I left in plenty of time, so Lewis Hamilton didn't need to worry that I might be taking his drive for the next F1 season. The bariatric unit had relocated and was now right next to the car park. Not 15 yards away from a whole row of parking – why oh why couldn't that have been the case when I needed it to be and not now when I could actually walk?

The grand moment arrived. I jumped on the scales. The numbers ticked up and up and I expected them to keep going but as if by some miracle they stopped. After a quick conversion from kilograms to stones, I worked out that since the assessment day I had lost just over six stone! Six stone in eight weeks. Do the maths! My God, that was quick. Six stone, that's the same as 38 bags of sugar. I'd certainly beaten that 40-stone barrier. In fact, I'd smashed it out of the stadium. I now weighed just – just! – 36 stone 12 pounds.

The check-up wasn't with the surgeon but with one of the nurses. She was pleased with the way my wounds were healing. I explained about the sickness problem I'd had which then seemingly solved itself. I outlined a typical daily food intake and bang! I found myself all finished. No problems, see you again in three months, Mr Bakewell. That was a damned sight easier than the last time I had been here.

I still couldn't quite believe the weight loss. It wasn't far off a stone a week. No doubt it would all slow down very quickly – after all, no one can lose weight that quickly for long. It was a fantastic start and got me thinking that the next goal had to be ten stone. A double-figure weight loss wasn't that far away.

Mum and Pete came to visit that weekend, and they were thrilled with the weight loss. Mum was even more thrilled with the fact that we went for a walk in the woods and that I could now walk for a distance without losing my breath. I showed them the spot of the infamous fall and related the story as if I'd spent ten days living out in the Siberian wilderness. I was pleased Mum was so thrilled with my progress. It must have been horrifying for my mother to see her only child almost self-destruct before her eyes. I must have put her through hell, but now I hoped over the following few years I'd make her happy and ease the burden that she had undoubtedly been carrying.

18

LONG HOT SUMMER

With six stone falling off so quickly, my clothes, which had started off literally fitting where they touched, were now becoming loose. I knew that I'd be going through new clothes extremely quickly and I didn't want to be buying brand-new stuff every other month. At the speed the weight was coming off, I'd have to remortgage the house in order to finance my shopping sprees. So I put off the thought of new clothes for as long as possible. When I finally got fed up with my tracksuit bottoms falling down every time I walked up the stairs, I realised I had to do something. So I decided to venture into our garage to find the old bags of gear that I had slung in there years ago in the forlorn hope that one day I'd be able to fit in them again. It seemed that day could be just around the corner.

Now, in many homes, going into the garage to find

something stored away is pretty much a stress-free experience. At Bakewell Towers, the garage resembled something out of an earthquake zone that had just been battered by a force 5 tornado and then made a bit more messy, just for good measure. The fact that the light bulb in there had smashed with the element still in the fitting so it couldn't be replaced just added to the excitement. Boxes were moved, bags examined and stray pieces of damaged garden furniture were lifted. Then I suddenly stopped dead in my tracks. And slowly it dawned on me. I was doing a physical job. I was on my feet, lifting and humping things about and I wasn't giving it a second thought. Just two months earlier, the thought of even having to walk downstairs and open the garage door would have been enough to bring me out in a sweat and make me reach for the nearest chair, but now – no problems.

The goal at the end of my quest, the bin bags of clothing, however, seemed to be elusive. I found things I hadn't seen for years: my bowls, a cello, a photograph of me with Ian Botham. And then I found them, under a discarded mattress in the corner, next to the Viking burial mound and the map to the lost city of El Dorado. I jest, but we do have some really old, useless crap stored in there – a task for the future, I think. The reunion with my old clothing was like meeting an old friend from school again. Initially, a little uncomfortable and then all of a sudden very familiar once again. These items were still a 7XL or a 6XL but I hadn't seen them for a long, long time. Shirts, tracksuit bottoms, T-shirts – a whole new wardrobe at my disposal. Then, at the bottom of the bag, there were some very unfamiliar items, three pairs of something made out of a strange, tough, hardwearing fabric. They were jeans. Jeans, the standard wardrobe item of any male under the age of 40. I hadn't worn any for probably going on five years. And shorts. Were my lovely legs about to get another airing?

I set about the task of trying the things on and every single item – apart from one pair of smart trousers that still had the label saying 58-inch waist and one pair of jeans – now fitted. I wasn't too upset about the trousers, it was obvious that they hadn't fitted me when I bought them in the first place and it would give me something to aim for. I even had some nice smart shirts in my new collection. So often in the past I have turned down opportunities to go places or attend events simply because I didn't have suitable clothing to wear. For the past three years, I had been dreading a wedding invite coming through the door. Let's face it, no one wants a fat bloke in a pair of green tracksuit bottoms at their wedding, do they?

The next new experience was a meal out with Jennie's mum at the Harvester restaurant. I knew this would be potentially difficult – what could I eat? The last thing I wanted was to have to rush to the toilets to be sick. It was as if I was having to learn everything all over again. I declined a visit to the salad cart and went for the straightforward spit-roast chicken and chips. 'Chips!' I hear you cry. Well, in reality, I still did have to eat some fat, the body can't use the fat on our bodies for its essential tasks. I had about two chips and some chicken and then proceeded to push my food round my plate in order to make it look like I was actually eating something. It was like I was five again and trying to hide the Brussels sprouts under the mashed potato! Obviously, I declined the pudding – sugar and gastric bypasses do not mix. Jennie's mum was horrified at the amount I was eating, thinking I was about to pass out at any moment. I explained that my diet wasn't a cause for concern as I had quite a few reserves to live on and I was getting enough to meet my needs. It was a good job I wasn't single. Any woman with whom I would have gone out to dinner on a romantic date would have thought me quite odd at the dinner table right then.

Summer was now well under way. I used to dread the summer months because of the heat, which I found intolerable. I'd always have the air conditioning up in the car to the point that ice would form on the inside of the windscreen. Windows would always be open in the office. Everyone else would be sitting there in jumpers and scarves and I would be in just my T-shirt. I would sweat even more than normal in summer and suffer a myriad of rashes, boils and nasty itches in the folds of my skin. But since the operation I had yet to be hot, never sweated and, more often than not, actually felt bloody cold. It may be that this year, I thought, I might actually welcome some sun on me.

And I did. I enjoyed walks on summer Sunday mornings and drinks outside on the long summer evenings. I worked in the garden. Yes. Worked in the garden. Weeding and planting stuff! I was like a child in a sweet shop, but without actually being able to eat the sweets, of course. It was like a whole new world of opportunity had opened up to me. The world was a big exciting place again, full of things to do and I wanted to do as much as I could. I was a big walking ball of excited energy, eager to sniff out the next challenge and the next step forward in my journey.

We went to Spain that summer for three long balmy weeks. We still drove – although I hoped that the following year it would be possible to actually fit in an airline seat and fly down there. With my new energy and the sleep apnoea resolved, it was a straight drive all the way through, all 1,200 miles of it. We left the UK for the tunnel at 5pm on the Wednesday and arrived at the apartment in Spain at about 8pm on the Thursday. I have to say I enjoy the drive, the ever-changing landscape of

France and then the Med road along the Spanish coast. The previous year's holiday to Mojacar in Spain had been something of a torment for me, but I was determined that on this one I would be more mobile and able to appreciate the heat.

If I wanted to be warm, then Spain was the place. Jennie and I sat on the patio together on the first night and watched the bushland, not three miles away, being consumed by the worst wild fires the area had seen for years. The heat wave, 43°C backed up by a hot, burning Saharan wind, fanned the fires, causing them to sweep out of all control. I sat and drank iced water and watched aircraft swoop down and drop gallons and gallons of water in an effort to extinguish the flames. By 2am, I thought we might have to pack our bags and evacuate, but the vegetation was very sparse for the last mile between the apartment and the fire and my fears proved unfounded. While it was horrifying, there was also something quite magical about watching the dancing orange flames high in the mountains in the dead of night, with the stars twinkling above. Sitting there, watching the stars got my mind thinking about the future and what I wanted to get out of life.

One of the things the hospital gave me before I was discharged was some information on the changes I might experience in my emotional state. The feelings and mindset I had in the past might change as my body changed around me. This change in mental attitude would, more often than not, not only affect the person who had the operation, but also their partner. Sometimes the partner struggles to accept the changes in the mindset of the 'fat' person that they once knew. Sometimes the person who has had the operation wants something new in their life. I personally felt that I had wasted quite a few years, and wanted to play catch-up.

It amazed me the difference between that holiday and just 12 months earlier. I was able to do so much more. The swimming pool in the apartment complex is all of 50 yards from the apartment, but last year it would take me two or even three 'stages' in order to walk the distance. This year I was almost running down there. Getting in and out of the pool was also a lot easier, plus I had more energy with which to actually swim. And it wasn't just spending time at the pool that was more pleasurable.

Jodie and her friend liked the beach. She was almost 16 so the boys on the beach generated more than just a passing interest. Hence the beach was a pretty standard port of call on a typical holiday day. Getting down to the sea, where everyone sat, was a far longer walk than the 50 yards to the pool. And walking on sand can be very energy-sapping. The previous year was a nightmare with me gasping for air and leaning on the umbrella; whereas this year I found it quite a pleasant stroll. Even getting in and out of the sea was easier. I remembered emerging from the Mediterranean 12 months previously only to find myself sinking into the wet sand where the sea met the beach. Poor Jennie had to rush to pull me out and virtually push me up the beach. This year, no such problem!

I was shocked that I could now do everything – walk around the shops to get the supplies from the supermarket, even go to restaurants in the evenings. There were still restrictions when it came to finding a suitable chair, but I had so many more options than before. Obviously, I couldn't eat very much but it didn't matter because I was back living in the real world once again. On occasions I had the cheek to order a child's meal. It did seem a little embarrassing at first. A strapping, 6ft 5in man tucking into two tiny sausages, mash and beans on a little plate with a cartoon on it. I certainly got some funny looks from the waiters. I got even funnier looks when I returned the plate with the meal only half-eaten Once, I got a nice little plastic car as my toy to go with the meal. I knew that there must be some benefits to all this.

Getting my head round the possibility that I really could leave food on my plate was a tough one. Normally, I would have been finishing every scrap of my own and then checking to see if there was anything being left by other people. I had to really think, Right, now I feel full, so it's time to stop eating. And I did. If only I could have done these things before the operation. There is no point in looking back and regretting mistakes in the past, because with hindsight you can change the world. It is best to think about the future and looking forward. That is what I did.

At the end of the holiday, I sat down with Jennie and told her that I had been thinking a lot and I had something important I had to discuss with her. So we sat down, talked and came to a decision.

19
BACK ON TRACK

I talked about life and the future. How I knew I had failed Jennie in the past and how I was determined to make up for it all now. How I felt guilty at not being able to give her another child and how, even if I did manage to shift massive amounts of weight, there would be no guarantee that my sperm count would shoot up. So we decided that we would seriously investigate adoption again. Our research a few years previously lead us to the conclusion that we would not fulfil the criteria simply because of my weight, so we had put the whole process on hold. Now it might well be worth getting things back on track.

Refreshed and inspired from our holiday in Spain, I decided I wanted to start doing some more exercise. So I rejoined the gym. I was looking at making changes to my regime so the rate at which I lost weight didn't slow as the volume of food I was eating increased. Obviously, over time, the amount of food I could eat would increase, otherwise I would never maintain a normal weight. I'd simply keep on dropping and dropping. My concern now was that I didn't want that slowing down to happen.

I didn't feel as intimidated going back in the gym as I thought I would. Something strange had happened. I seemed to stop getting the stares from people. Whenever I went out before, people would stare, point and whisper behind their hands. Now no one really gives me a second glance. Children do still sometimes stare up at me, but it's more now in awe of my height and stature than simply because I was very fat. The weight had really come off my upper torso. My face, my shoulders and my chest had all shrunk considerably, causing my body to become quite an odd shape as I was still very big round the middle. But now I wasn't feeling smothered by my size. It was also amazing how much a change in body shape affected how I felt about my clothing. Things were again becoming way too big – with the reduction in my shoulders and my chest, the sleeves on many of my T-shirts were coming down to my mid-forearm. Some of them began to resemble dresses.

The instructors at the gym were all really friendly and helped me adapt to my ever-changing needs. I was going back to the gym of which I had been a member before.

It was a great place because it also had a swimming pool and I thought I would get some good use out of that as well as the gym. I started off very slowly, becoming familiar with the equipment once again. I did six minutes walking up a hill on the treadmill, six minutes on the recumbent bike, six minutes on the normal stationary bike and then a final six minutes on the arm bike. I also did a little bit of weight work to tone myself up as I went along. It was hardly Olympic-level training but once again it was forcing my body to adjust and adapt to new things and hopefully to lose more weight.

My next appointment was coming up at St Richard's so there was another weigh-in on the horizon. It was now the middle of August, some five-and-a-half months after the operation. I hoped that I would break past that ten-stone weight-loss barrier which would truly be a remarkable achievement in such a short period of time. But I was worried that, as the amount I could now eat was increasing, the desire to eat was following suit. After the operation, I had no real desire for food, no hunger. But now that feeling was creeping back. I was not only eating more in one sitting but also eating more regularly.

So it was with some trepidation that I stood once more on the scales at St Richard's. Eleven-and-a-half stone lost. Wow. Better than I had thought. The dietician was even worried that I might not be eating enough and told me to make sure that I either had some toast with cheese or a yoghurt before going to bed. This would help me keep up my protein intake. This was something else I was also getting more wary of. I felt that maybe I was eating too much carbohydrate. For breakfast I normally had cornflakes and half a glass of milk; lunch would be a sandwich, then potatoes at tea and more toast before bed. But the weight was still coming off at a fair old pace so I guess with this level of carb intake there was nothing to be worried about. In fact, the weight might even have been coming off too quickly, we are talking about more than two stone a month, that's over half a stone a week – some rapid loss.

The rapid nature of the weight loss was having a visible effect on my body. I could feel that in a number of areas skin was starting to go saggy. The tops of my arms for one, giving me the start of the dreaded bingo wings. My armpits also seemed to drop. Skin that was once up under my arm, in the pit region, was now down to just above my waist. It seemed to flap about when I stood up from the kitchen chair and would slap back down again, making a highly embarrassing slapping sound like being struck with a wet haddock. Then there was my once impressive pair of double-D man boobs which seemed to have shrunk to closer to a B-cup, now hovering somewhere around my waist. The fat was now also starting to shift round the stomach. My enormous stomach had been quite firm with compacted fat; now it was very wobbly indeed.

I had lost so much weight from my waist that my trousers kept falling down. This time it was my jeans that were proving to be the problem. When I put things like my mobile phone and wallet in the pockets, the weight of them started to pull my jeans down. This wasn't good because my 8XL undercrackers had long been consigned to the dustbin. Quite frankly, I wasn't prepared to buy new ones every single month and decided to go commando until the weight loss had stabilised, so as not to waste money on pants that would only be good for a few weeks. After an incident in the local garage when filling up for petrol might have resulted in a prison sentence for indecent exposure, I thought I needed to dig out the smaller pair of jeans that hadn't fitted when I liberated my clothing from the garage. I hunted high and low for the bloody things for a good hour – could I find them? Could I hell! Then I realised something. I was actually wearing them and didn't even realise. It was the smaller pair that was too small. Fortunately, as part of my hunting, I had found a belt that hadn't fitted me for a long, long time. I put this on the jeans and found that I had to make extra holes in it over a foot from the end.

Little things like this really helped motivate me and kept me pushing to the next level. My training stepped up a notch in the gym. I started doing 20 minutes on the treadmill and ten minutes on the bike. I even started having a little go on the rowing machine. All of this was really helping increase my fitness levels. OK, I wasn't ready for the NASA astronaut programme just yet, but I was more than capable of walking wherever I liked.

The back pains I had been getting after the operation had now mostly cleared up. I did still sometimes get pain when driving for a while, but it was something I could live with. Maybe the pain had disappeared because I hardly ever stayed still. Whereas before the operation I would plan things so I would have to do the least amount of standing or walking, now I would take things as they came and this often resulted in me rushing up and down the stairs a lot. Although stairs were still one thing I wasn't very confident on, I felt I had trouble with my balance. And I was so scared of falling down them when I was at my heaviest that I continued to treat them gingerly. For as long as I can remember, at the back of my mind was the fear that my knees would buckle under me. I hoped that, as the months passed without incident, confidence would return.

The issue with my balance was a little bit odd and a lot disconcerting. It was as though I was adapting to a change in my centre of gravity. I'd trip up over the smallest possible, highly unlikely item. It was as though chair legs would suddenly move as I was walking past or tables would leap out into my path. I never actually fell over, but would stumble about, prompting shouts of 'bumbling fool!' from Jennie. I simply put it down to becoming used to my new body; after all, I wasn't used to moving with this degree of regularity or this pace. Whenever I would leap up out of a chair or the bed, I'd be a little bit dizzy. The room would start to spin and I'd start rocking all over the place. Again, I put this down to a combination of a lack of food and my body adjusting to my newfound sprightliness, it was something that I had to be aware of and watch for the future.

Jennie had received two pieces of news. Firstly, she had rung the adoption people and after a long chat about the process we were advised to apply in the New Year. That way I would have lost more weight and Jennie would also have had her gastric bypass operation and also be on the losing side. The people at the council were very helpful and they talked for about half an hour. Jennie was honest about the weight issues and was able to explain that, because we were tackling them head-on, they didn't need to be a cause for concern. The adoption people at the council even asked, 'Do you want one or two children?' So in a matter of months a whole new chapter to our lives would begin. The second piece of good news was that Jennie had finally received her date for a consultation at St Richard's.

Jennie, like me, had suffered with her weight, although nowhere near to the same degree that I had. After getting me through the operation, she had started the process to have a bypass. Because her BMI was a lot lower than mine, she had to go and see the dietician at the hospital for six months before St Richard's agreed to a consultation. When her referral letter arrived, to say she was ecstatic is an understatement. Unlike me, she would gladly have gone down to theatre that very afternoon. If we could now get Jennie sorted out as well, that would be fantastic progress as we could continue the rest of the journey together, supporting each other, although this time the roles would be reserved and it would be me that would have all the worry and all the stress. Having someone you love go under the knife is far harder than undergoing the process yourself.

One thing that had certainly changed in the last six months was the increase in my levels of confidence. When you are very fat, every single ounce of self-confidence is drained from you, like squeezing a sponge dry. You feel worthless and useless on so many different levels. Physically, emotionally, intellectually, sexually – the list could simply go on and on. But bit by bit the confidence creeps back, slowly at first and then you get a little bit of a swagger again.

Physically, you feel so much better and you begin to lose that feeling of vulnerability. Vulnerability is a strange word to use. But even when I was so large, I was very exposed because of my physical condition. It's hard to grasp the concept of an elephant being as weak as a newborn deer, but that is how I'd describe it. Thinking back to that day I wanted to attend the cricket match, I was a walking victim, hobbling along the road, sweating, gasping for breath and stopping for a lean every 15 yards. I was basically shouting out, 'Come and mug me, please.' When you know that you aren't able to protect your family, you do feel so useless. There is also the fear that, if I tripped over, how on earth would I be able to stand up again? If the car crashed, how would I be able to get out? All these things play on your mind, you stop doing things and that all-important confidence drains away.

Emotionally, I was all over the place. As a super morbidly obese man, my failings and weaknesses constantly played on my mind, which leaves few resources to fight the depression. As that depression takes hold, it drags you deeper and deeper down into a dark, dark place. And yet you try to hold on to things that you remember in the past, how things could be positive again, which gnaws away at you. That classic quote from the John Cleese film *Clockwise* leaps to mind: 'I can handle the despair, it's the hope I can't stand.'

Obviously, the reduction in your ability to function sexually is very damaging, not just for yourself but for your partner, too. The fact that you aren't sexually attractive any more hurts deeply, which further harms your emotional state and takes you further down the slippery slide of depression. We are sexual animals first and foremost, and to deny this aspect of our personalities is deeply damaging.

All of these things hammer your confidence until none is left and you are just a shell of your former self. I count a regain in my confidence as just as important as the health benefits from the weight loss. By losing the weight, I have gained so much.

20
GOING BACK BUT GOING FORWARD

Jennie's operation date came round really quickly, so before I knew it I was heading back to the hospital, but in the other position, and wondering whether I would be able to cope under this different sort of pressure.

I can't say I had been particularly nervous about Jennie's impending operation. I'd been there, done that and got the smaller T-shirt, but when we arrived back at the hospital for her pre-op assessment everything changed. It was like watching the whole process again through different eyes. I realised that when I had my operation I had the easy job of simply lying down on the operating table and going to sleep. It was everyone else who had all the worry and all the stress when I was quite happily in the land of nod. This time I'd be doing the waiting.

What was very useful about Jennie having her operation at the same place was that, whenever we were at the clinic for appointments related to her procedure, I could weigh myself as well. It was early November, just over eight months since my operation. I was a little worried about what the scales would show. I knew that the weight loss would start to slow down at some point as it was impossible to keep going at two stone a month forever. I also knew that I had certainly begun to eat more. This was nothing that shouldn't have happened by this stage, but doubts were always in the back of my mind. It's fair to say that I was pleasantly surprised when I got on the scales to see that I had lost 15 stone. The 30-stone barrier had now been broken, and I was clocking in at just 28 stone. This meant that at the very most I only had another ten stone to lose. Quite possibly I'd be happy with another eight stone off to level out at 20 stone.

My appearance had changed quite significantly. My face and neck were as if a new man was looking at me in the mirror. Bizarrely, when I was at my heaviest, I found my face extremely difficult to shave, I don't know why, I can't explain it. But the razor blade just wouldn't glide across the skin, leaving me always looking a scruff-bag. But now, with the skin tighter to the bone, I can get a really nice close shave. A little point maybe, but something that makes all the difference to confidence and feelings of self-worth. I was losing weight, but gaining all sorts of things, a jawline being one of them. The other day I found out I even had ribs.

It was quite amusing in Jennie's pre-op assessment. The nurses and dieticians were running through their list with Jennie, while looking at me with more attention than is usual for the patient's partner. It was obvious that they thought they recognised me, but weren't quite sure. We had to keep on explaining that I'd been in March and had now lost 15 stone. Everyone was very impressed with my progress, so much so that Jennie got more than a little bit annoyed that it was me who was getting all the attention. Thankfully, everything was good on her assessment; she only weighed in at 22 stone so nothing at all like mine. Fortunately, the anaesthetist wrote on her form 'Very Low Risk'.

Fifteen stone! Just shy of two stone a month. I really couldn't complain with that sort of weight loss. I'd love to shift that other ten stone, but, in all honesty, if the weight loss dried up now, I'd still be happy – I've got my life back. When I think back at all those years of fighting this seemingly never-ending battle, this solution is just amazing. My route to the summit was a long hard one. I'd tried many roads to get there, none of which worked out for me. But once I found the right path, I saw that the peak was in sight and that nothing, absolutely nothing, could stop me from conquering it.

EVERYTHING TO LOSE

I understand that there will be people who say that I took the 'easy' way out. With the greatest respect to those who think that – bollocks! My life, for almost as long as I can remember, has been a constant struggle against obesity. I've tried everything I possibly could have done in order to lose weight. But when you are addicted to food, then nothing works – apart from this surgery. Anyone who thinks that I took an easy way should try living in my condition for just a day. They should feel the frustration, the self-loathing and the despair. They should try to move about and do normal, everyday things such as getting up from a chair, and when they do they should feel the pressure on the spine, the pain in the knees and that desperate gasping for breath. They should squeeze into a tiny chair in a sleep disorder clinic and be told that the previous night you almost died by stopping breathing 386 times. And they should feel the piercing stares of disgusted people on them; they should hear the whispered insults, mocking laughter and see the finger-pointing. And then, after they have experienced this, they need to go home to their sanctuary and fill their faces with food because it is the only solution they know to all their problems. Finally, they need to live for almost six months in fear of dying on the operating table and then they need to take that long, short walk to the theatre and say goodbye to the person they love, not knowing if they will ever see them again. Only after doing all that can they say it was the 'easy' route.

Jennie did very well on the milk diet. After a rocky start (during the first weekend, I honestly thought that she would soon be tucking into fish and chips and sticky toffee pudding), ten days soon passed and, bang, here we were again 'Operation Day'. No repeat of my miscalculated timing on this occasion, and hence no need to repeat my Lewis Hamilton impression. Therefore, we arrived on time and without additional stress. As is typical after a long car journey, we both needed the loo before going up to the ward. There was a man waiting downstairs in the reception area who was looking very nervous and was obviously there for the operation. He looked at me and smiled.

'I saw you on telly last night,' he said.

'You did,' I confirmed.

Strangely, the documentary about me was screened only the previous night. As I had vowed, I hadn't watched it, but Jennie said that it showed me in a good light. It turns out my story had made this guy feel very positive about his surgery today, so for me that was a good enough reason for participating in the filming and opening up my life to the cameras.

Up on the ward, Jennie settled into her bed and went about having the pre-op tests and the now familiar rounds of form filling. She had lost 13 pounds in the previous ten days, not bad at all for a lady her size. Of course, all the nurses recognised me and again I received some great comments about my progress so far. It was nice to see the people who cared so well for me again, but I was very conscious that this was Jennie's day, so I tried to stay in the background as much as possible. Jennie was second on the list, which meant that she had a bit of a wait before she went down to theatre. This was something that I hadn't had to cope with and, as time ticked slowly, I could feel her getting more and more nervous. I was pretty calm and trying to be a rock for Jennie.

Finally, the call came and we walked down the same corridors I had done eight months previously. Once again, when we came to say goodbye, Jennie was in tears. I held it together and got out quick so she could pull herself together before going into the theatre.

Now all I could do was wait. I walked around the hospital, and finally found the canteen. I had the world's worst sandwich and then started to phone people to say that she had gone down to theatre to keep my mind occupied. I walked – no, paced – the corridors some more and then went to try to shut my eyes in the car. I was still holding it together pretty well as I waited. The surgeon (not the same one as I'd had) had promised to ring me on the mobile when Jennie was out, so I was desperate for the phone to ring. Then Jodie rang up, in tears, panicking about her mum. How I wished that it was me on the table fast sleep, rather than having to go through all this heart-wrenching waiting. Then, finally, some three-and-a-half hours after I had said goodbye, I got the call to say that everything was OK. I almost burst into tears. I rang Jodie and Jennie's mum to put them out of their agony. The surgeon had said that Jennie would be about an hour and a half in recovery before coming back on to the ward, so I went and paced the corridors a little more. God knows how far I walked that day!

I waited and saw that Jennie was doing well and then, some 14 hours after getting up, started the two-hour drive home. I was never more relieved to get to my bed than that night, I was well and truly shattered. It's so true that worrying about someone is so much worse than having to go through it yourself. If I hadn't had my own operation, I wouldn't have been able to do what I did that day. I simply wouldn't have had the energy or the levels of fitness to keep myself wired for so long and I certainly wouldn't have been able to pace the corridors as I had.

If I had to choose just one benefit of the surgery, then it would have to be the regaining of my mobility. Until it has gone, you simply don't understand what you have lost. It took me quite a while to realise that I was able to do so many things again. Jennie had to keep pushing me and reminding me that I didn't have 'fatitis' any more. Physically, I may well be so much better, but I did find it very hard to get out of the mindset that I had been in for so long. The feeling that you can't do anything and that you don't want to do anything – resisting this has been the biggest challenge.

Am I still addicted to food? The answer, I believe, is still yes. After all, I have only had a physical procedure, not a psychological one. But now, I don't need as much food to satisfy the cravings. I can't eat some of the 'bad' foods because they make me ill. So ultimately my condition is 'managed'. Am I cured? No, not yet, but my dependency on my drug is greatly reduced.

So, what now, what does the future hold? I don't have a crystal ball, but I see myself losing that next ten stone. I feel that it will be harder. Maybe I need a challenge in order to help me achieve it, something that I would never have even dreamed of before. A marathon maybe, or swimming the Channel, or possibly an assault on Mount Everest or joining the NASA space programme to be the first man on Mars. Maybe I'm getting carried away. But one thing is certain, I feel that so much of my life has been wasted trying to beat this terrible addiction and its devastating effects that I'm determined to make the most of every single moment I have.

GOING BACK BUT GOING FORWARD

As I go and pick up Jennie from hospital to take her home to complete her recovery, I know that the next steps on our road to healthier, longer and most importantly happier life will be taken together.

Do you want to transform your life and feel the benefit of change?

As a thank you for buying this book, you can get Neil's new ten day Change your Life Programme – which can be applied to any aspect of your life – for free.

Simply visit www.changeyourlifeintendays.com

Neil now talks to businesses, schools and youth groups about his experiences with his inspirational message 'Everything to Gain'

To arrange for Neil to speak at your event, visit www.neilbakewell.com or email mail@neilbakewell.com